SAFARI PRESS

Backtracking

Backtracking

I.T. Taylor

Safari Press Inc.

P. O. Box 3095, Long Beach,California 90803, USA

Taylor, I. T.

First edition

Safari Press Inc.

1998, Long Beach, California

ISBN 1-57157-103-5

Library of Congress Catalog Card Number: 97-69552

10 9 8 7 6 5 4 3 2 1

Contents

Acknowledgments

I would be remiss if I did not acknowledge the extraordinary effort made by three ladies who made this book possible: Marcy Worsham and Cyndi Wendt Sykora edited my drivel into the finished form you now see, and Jeanne Byerly of C-T Typing in Victoria, Texas, literally tamed a bushel basket of loose scribblings and fed them into her computer.

Finally there is also the little gray-headed lady, Billye, who has lived with me through all the stories of the past forty-six years. When at least fifty publishers throughout the United States turned my book down because it did not fit into one of their niches, she simply stated, "THIS BOOK WILL BE PUBLISHED." Enough said!

This book is dedicated to

my granddaughters

Dawn, Andi, Chrissy, Becky, and Debby

May there be a place left for them

to go to be lonely.

Harking In

Many years ago I bred a dandy Walker foxhound bitch to a fine Goodman foxhound. Distemper left me only one pup from a thirteen-pup litter. This pup started running on the first fox he ever smelled. As a yearling pup he would stay in the long hard coyote race and get his part of the race. Before the age of two he would go to a barking wolf and make him run. Good training? Shoot! All the training that pup ever got was how to load and unload. He was a natural-born hunter.

I once took a litter of Black and Tan pups out of a fine bitch and a good dog. I kept and hunted four of these pups. All four would open on a coon trail before they were four months old, would tree just after they were four months old, and treed a coon by themselves before they were six months old. Good training? All I did was open the gate and let those pups out of the dog pen. They were born coonhounds.

A few years back I bred a nice beagle bitch to an even better beagle dog. Six of the eight-dog litter made good hounds. I ran two in my pack for years, a dog and a bitch, and I considered them really fine rabbit hounds. Either of these hounds would find a rabbit, jump him and run him until he was caught or holed. The bitch would tree a holed rabbit better than many tree dogs. Good training? All I ever did was walk them into the brush.

I was born in 1928. My mother was a hunter, and she was from a family of hunters. They were hound men, fishermen, bird hunters, and riflemen. My daddy was a hunter. He was a meat hunter as opposed to a sportsman. He fed a big family with a battered, old single-shot shotgun. When he went hunting, he produced meat.

I started hunting and fishing as soon as I could slip away from the house. That was when I was about five years old, and I hunted with a slingshot. Did I receive good training as a hunter? Man, I have had to fight to get to hunt my whole life. I cannot remember a time before I was a grown man that I was encouraged to hunt. It did not make any difference though, because like the dogs I described above, I was born and bred to hunt. There has never been a time when I thought I was as good a hunter as the pups I talked about, but like them, I have only been responding to a drive that was put into me by my pedigree. My pedigree reads like this:

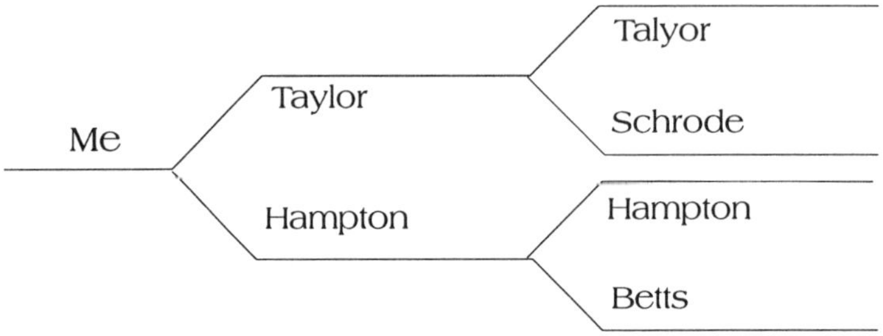

I think I would have been a better hunter but that Taylor in the third generation, Old Frank, was not a hunter. I am careful not to breed my hounds with a weakness like that in their pedigree.

If I look deep within myself I have to confess that I am probably more of a hound man than I am a gun hunter or a fisherman. Be that as it may, any form of hunting thrills me as much today as it did fifty years ago. It is a fact that stalking a fox in the pasture back of my house and watching it catch a squirrel to eat, excites me as much as stalking and killing a good mule deer in Idaho. In the past fifty years I have crossed paths with many hundreds of hound men, runners of coonhounds, foxhounds, rabbit hounds, coyote hounds, bobcat hounds and mountain lion hounds. Also, in those fifty years I have never met a hound man who ever amounted to anything when judged by the standards of our society. If one gives the attention to a pack of hounds that they require to make them good and keep them good, then one has little time to pursue the goals of our modern society—money, power, and, prestige. I like to think of myself as a hound man.

Since I am certain that our expanding civilization will rob future generations of being able to hunt as I have enjoyed it, I would like to describe hunting as I have known it for the past sixty years.

It pleases me to think that some young person with a hunting pedigree, at some future date, would look at this to see what hunting was like, way back then.

Now I am going to spin a series of yarns that cover a good portion of my hunting life. I would be more comfortable if I could tell these stories around a campfire and over a pot of fresh coffee, but since that is not possible I will have to make do with what I have.

Bear in mind that hunters are notorious liars. Also keep in mind that different people can see the same event from different perspectives. To the best of my ability I have stayed as close to the bare truth, as I remember it, as is possible for an old hunter to do.

Also keep in mind that I have probably subconsciously tried to make me appear to be smarter, stronger, faster, or better than I really am.

Just to show how distorted my view of myself is, let me relate to you this experience. A few years ago I was given a picture of me taken without my knowledge in an Idaho wilderness area. In my mind's eye I pictured myself as young, handsome, tall, broad shouldered, and straight. The picture showed a small, scrawny, big nosed, stoop-shouldered, crooked necked, swaybacked, old man standing there with his hands in his pockets holding up his britches that wanted to slip off his butt.

Odds are that I have the same distorted opinion of my mental and my hunting abilities.

Sounds

It must have been early in the fall when I was twelve that I decided I was big enough to go to the river by myself and spend the night fishing. The Lavaca River was about four miles from our place, and I talked "The Old Man" into dropping me and my gear off at a low-water bridge crossing of the river. My gear consisted of ten fishhooks, a ball of cotton cord, a bull's-eye kerosene lantern, a frying pan, a pocketknife, some kitchen matches, an old quilt, a flour sack filled with a corner off a side of home-cured bacon, and some stale biscuits.

The site I chose for my camp was down the river several hundred yards from the low-water bridge crossing. There was a nice, level, shady spot on the bank right at the head of some good looking fishing water. I dragged up a supply of good, sound, dry wood for my fire, spread out my quilt, and found a limb from which to hang my lantern. Camp was ready.

Then I looked over my fishing hole and decided where to set my hooks. I put out all ten hooks on individual drop lines that were secured to overhanging willow limbs. My next priority was bait, and I had decided to have as much variety as possible.

I tore up a big rotten log and secured a couple of huge grub worms. Then a search of ice weeds yielded a couple of fat, yellow grasshoppers. I hooked the worms and the grasshoppers on part of my drop lines. Next I cut a long willow switch and started walking up the riverbank. In a short distance I was able to whack several spring frogs with my switch, which stunned them enough for me to catch them. I hooked the frogs on some of the lines. A couple of hundred yards from my camp was a slew that held floodwater from the river. Due to dry conditions, the water in the slew was very shallow. I stripped off my clothes and with my feet I churned that slew water up into a muddy mess. In a few minutes small perch were gasping at the top of the water for oxygen. I scooped up some in my hands and baited lines with them. By this time it was less than an hour before dark.

You can talk about a good feeling of confidence, pride, and well-being, but until you have made your own first overnight camp, set out your own set of fishing lines, secured a variety of bait for your lines, and realized that you can get more bait anytime you want it, then you probably have no understanding of what that good feeling really is.

The temperature was almost perfect. The day was just cool enough so that the sunshine felt good. The night promised to be much cooler, but I was confident that my campfire and quilt would offer me all the comfort I wanted.

I built up a small campfire and sliced up half of my slab of bacon. I fried the bacon to a golden brown in my skillet. Then I cut open half my stale biscuits and fried them in the bacon grease. A thick hunk of home-cured bacon between two halves of crisply fried, stale biscuit may not be your idea of gourmet eating, but if it isn't then you probably have never feasted on it. The only problem was that the salty bacon made me thirsty, but that was no problem because right there beside my camp was the Lavaca River filled with fine drinking water. Think about it for a second. On that fall day in 1940 the Lavaca River was a typical small Texas river that had no agricultural pollution from insecticides, herbicides, or fungicides, no industrial waste from any source, and no human waste. That water had a wonderful flavor with just a hint of willow leaves and was best drunk as it riffled over a shallow sandy bottom.

Just before dark I fired up my bull's-eye kerosene lantern, which for your information, is the sorriest light source ever invented. Since my campfire had died down, I also stirred it up and added a few fresh sticks. An old owl hooted with a loud, screaming call not far from my camp. I jumped a foot when he broke the silence. The skin prickled on the back of my neck. I got the lantern and ran my fishing lines. My expectations were high, so it was a big letdown when I discovered that not even any bait was missing. I went back to camp to the serenade of a whole chorus of owls scattered up and down the river. Their constant *who-who-whoing* made me more than a little nervous.

I punched up the fire and added a few new limbs. As the fresh wood caught fire, it enlarged the small circle of light furnished by the lantern. The additional light was a real comfort, and it did seem to ward off some of the effects of the owl hoots.

As it got darker and darker, I began to notice a great variety of noises. Something was stirring around in the dead leaves just a short distance from camp. I kept telling myself it was only an armadillo, as I added more limbs to the fire. Something big boldly slogged down to the river. Reason told me that it was an old cow getting a drink but in my mind I really was not certain that it was. I got out my pocketknife and opened the best blade. It was sort of a comfort. As a reflex action I added a few more limbs to the fire to help ward off the ever-increasing noises.

I decided it was time to run my lines again. My bait was not disturbed, so I made my way back to camp in the minimal light furnished by the bull's-eye lantern. That crackling fire sure looked good when I reached camp. It was colder now, so I pulled the quilt up around me. The warmth furnished by the quilt and the fire made me relaxed and drowsy.

I awoke with a start. A couple of animals were having a terrible fight on the riverbank in the area where my lines were set. I listened to the growls, squeals, and squalls from the fight with my heart thumping in my throat.

Flinging off my quilt, I tore headlong for home. Limbs, twigs, vines, and thorns tore at me as I fled desperately in the dark. Within a quarter of a mile I was totally winded. I still struggled on toward home, even if my pace was greatly slowed. Several times I was sure I could hear something behind me. I felt for my knife, but it was back in camp. I continued to fight my way through the thick brush. After a while I broke free of the brush and was out in open pastureland. I knew that there was a high line that crossed the back of our place and continued on across the river close to where I was camped. I made my way toward it and finally was able to skylight it. I turned down the high line and at a long trot headed home.

When I got to the house, the lights were out and everyone was in bed. I slipped into the house and crawled into bed. I awoke to the smell of bacon and coffee. It was a tough trip to the kitchen knowing that I would have to face Momma and Daddy. No one said a word when I sat down and started eating.

After breakfast I just said that I was going back to the river to get my gear. After an hour's walk I was back in camp. Everything was just as I had left it, except my campfire was burned out and my lantern was out of fuel. I made a bundle of everything rolled up in the quilt. Then I went to retrieve my fishing lines.

I thought that was a good fishing hole. When I got close enough, I could see three of the willow limbs bobbing to the tug of a hooked fish. In my excitement I jumped into the river fully dressed to retrieve my catch. One of the big grub lines yielded a nice channel catfish. One of the grasshopper hooks had caught a small channel catfish. And one of my perch lines had a dandy yellow catfish. I secured my catch on a short piece of fishing line, rolled up my fishing lines on a stick, retrieved my bundle of camp gear, and went home.

It was fried catfish, fried potatoes, homemade light bread, homemade ketchup, and sliced onion for supper that night. Those catfish sure tasted good. One of the great surprises of my life was that no one ever said a word about me getting scared out of the woods.

I know I never mentioned it, that is not until some twenty-five years later, when Momma and I had a good laugh about it one night. She told me that Daddy had heard me come in during the night and had told her not to say anything as I would probably be feeling pretty low.

Sounded to me like "The Old Man" had gone down the same trail I had traveled. He probably let a couple of boar coons run him out of a river bottom too.

I have never heard an owl hoot since then that I have not, in my mind, gone back to my first camp on the Lavaca River. In fifty years it has become a most pleasant trip.

A Hard Straight Shooter

Momma and Daddy were gone for the day. I had been waiting for this opportunity for weeks. My plan was to shoot Dad's old, single-shot, 12-gauge shotgun. I was eleven years old, and I sure did not want to wait until I was twelve to shoot that gun.

I got the gun out from behind the back door. I knew that it would be loaded, but I checked just to make sure. Then I examined it closely. It had Diamond Arms Co., St. Louis, stamped on the receiver and Choke Bored stamped on the barrel. There was not any reference to the gauge of the gun. I know now that it was an Iver Johnson and that some hardware company had it made under their trademark. The buttstock on it was as crooked as a dog's hind leg with enough drop for two shotguns. Many were the tales I had heard about the fierce kick the gun had. I had also heard a number of tales about how hard it shot. It was Dad's sole gun, and its purpose was to put meat on the table. Dove, quail, ducks, geese, squirrel, plover, and snipe were common fare for both the gun and our table.

I went out back looking for something to shoot. About that time I heard a woodpecker in a mulberry tree out by the stock trough. I made a cautious stalk, and I knew I was in range when I spotted the flicker. Then I got to thinking about the kick of that shotgun. I remembered a tale Dad told about it kicking him over as he squatted in some weeds and shot at some geese flying over. Then I got inspiration as to how to control the kick.

I backed my right shoulder up against a hackberry tree. I lightly held the gun to my shoulder. I squinted down the barrel and got the flicker lined up. I touched her off. *Whee doggies*! Thought I had been kicked by a mule and had an anvil dropped on me at the same time. Blood was pouring all over the front of my shirt from the blow of the stock as it recoiled into my nose. The pain from the compression of my shoulder between the stock in front and the tree in back made me drop the gun. I finally stopped the flow of blood from my nose. I took off my shirt to rinse it out in the stock tank. There was a bloody spot in the area where I had leaned against the tree bark. When I finished rinsing the shirt, I took it to the house, gave it a washing with a bar of soap and the rub board, and hung it out to dry. Then I went back and got the shotgun, reloaded it, and put it behind the door. My next action was to examine myself in the mirror. Found a blue lump on the right cheek under my eye. The front of my shoulder was blue where the buttstock recoiled into it. The back of my shoulder where I leaned against the tree was a mess with purple puncture marks over a blue area as large as my hand. About this time I noticed that the swelling and blue from the lump on my cheek was spreading to my eye.

Started racking my brain about the story to tell my folks to explain my condition. I do not know to this day if I got the flicker. I do know that I got a fresh hobby out of the deal that has lasted to this day. It is called, "curing an incurable flinch."

Must have been at least a week before I thought about shooting a gun again. The problem was that many of my friends were getting guns, mostly .22 rifles, to shoot. I wanted a gun of my own in the worst kind of a way but "The Old Man" issued a flat "No!" when I asked about a .22. After I had broached the subject many times over the next months he finally relented and told me that I could have a shotgun. I could have it, that is, when I had the money to pay for it.

Money was the thing I had in shortest supply. I did not receive an allowance. I did not get paid for work done at home. I was kept too busy at home to be able to have jobs like mowing lawns in town. My prospects for having the money to pay for a shotgun were bleak indeed.

At this time in our history Japan was buying scrap iron from the United States. Japan used our scrap iron to prepare their war machine for World War II. For a number of years in the late 1930s it stimulated a bristling business in all areas of our country. Capitalist that I was, by necessity, and recognizing opportunity when it knocked, I set forth on my first economic venture, selling scrap iron.

I asked Dad what he planned to do with the junk farm machinery scattered around our place. He responded that he had no plans for it. I asked if I could have it. He answered that I could but not to bother him with it. I started accumulating a pile of my valuable material down close to the barn. Cultivator parts, big iron wheels, a mower sickle bar, the head off of some large engine, the engine from a Model T Ford, a cracked wash pot, a box of old nuts and bolts, window sash weights, pieces of pipe, let me tell you nothing was too large or too small for my pile of goodies.

At my first opportunity I went to Arnold's Hardware Store in Edna to look at their shotguns. Would you believe they had just the gun I wanted, a Stevens 20-gauge, single shot with a full choke barrel. Every time I went to town I went by and looked at that shotgun. They even let me handle it every once in a while. Oh, how I wanted that gun.

My next problem was getting my scrap iron into town. Daddy had a black man come to mow the pasture. He came with his mower hooked behind his wagon. I made a deal with him to haul my whole pile of assets into town for me on his wagon. I think he charged me fifty cents to be paid after I sold the junk. He even helped me to load some of the larger pieces.

I remember that Kennedy's Blacksmith Shop was buying scrap iron. If memory serves, my scrap iron was weighed on a cotton scale and that I received a penny a pound for it. I took my $7.25, paid off my hauling debt and left in a hurry to Arnold's Hardware with my remaining $6.75 burning a hole in my pocket.

There was a little man who worked at Arnold's. I think his name was Nowlan. He was short and stout with a big, round, bald head. He always wore thick glasses and a friendly smile. I asked him about the 20-gauge shotgun. I felt horrible when he explained that the gun had been sold.

He reached up and handed me another gun from the rack. It was a 16-gauge made by the Diamond Arms Co. and its barrel was full choke. There was a rubber recoil pad on a good straight stock. Strange as it may seem, the perforations in the recoil pad were in the form of our cattle brand, repeated over and over, I remarked that I was afraid of the recoil of a 16-gauge. Mr. Nowlan replied that it was little more than that of a 20-gauge. I held my breath and asked how much the gun was. Mr. Nowlan asked if Daddy was going to buy the gun for me. I replied that Dad had given permission for me to buy the gun but that I had sold scrap iron for the money. He asked how much money I had. I told him $6.75. Mr. Nowlan folded his little short arms over his chest and squinted at me through his thick glasses. He finally said I sure was lucky because that was just how much they wanted for the gun. He took my money. I left town for home at fast as I could run. Boy, that shotgun felt good swinging in my right hand as I ran. Was not until years later that I stopped to realize that shotguns did not sell for that price at that time. That sweet little old man, Mr. Nowlan, knew how badly I wanted that gun. He knew I would be years getting enough money to pay the full price. I am willing to bet he hardly got his cost out of it.

Well, that was just one of my many sweet experiences while growing up in a small Texas town in the 1930s and 1940s.

When I reached home it suddenly dawned on me that I did not have any ammunition for the new gun. Not only that but I could see no way that I would be able to buy any in the near future. Momma told me to just hold still for a minute. She went upstairs and rummaged around in an old trunk of hers. After a bit she came out of that trunk with three 16-gauge shells. She said that they had belonged to one of her brothers. I have no idea why she had them in her trunk but I know they would have to had been there since before I was born.

I did not linger around giving thanks or looking a gift horse in the mouth. I left for our creek bottom squirrel hunting. The first one I found was close to Branch's barn. I was pretty close when I spotted him. I held dead on and touched off my shot. Hardly felt the recoil and could you believe I blew that squirrel half in two. You talk about a hard shooting shotgun! Hunted awhile longer and spotted another squirrel peeping at me over a limb. Again I was pretty close and this shot took off the top of his head. I took my two squirrels home and dressed them, saving my last shell. I asked Momma to cook them for supper. I sure was proud of my gun. It did not kick too bad and I for certain knew it shot straight and hard.

That night at supper when Daddy asked where the squirrel came from, you think I failed to tell him? Shoot!

Meat Hunter or Sportsman

A shotgun is absolutely of no value if one does not have ammunition for it. That was the sorry state of affairs I found myself faced with after I finally was able to buy my first shotgun.

Someone told me that Sprung's Grocery would buy pecans. I checked with them and sure enough they were buying. They were paying a penny a pound for them. I knew where there were some big pecan trees on the Lavaca River.

The next Saturday, after I had finished my work around the house, I was given the afternoon off. I crawled up on my horse Skinflint. I did not have a saddle at that time, and went to the Lavaca River. I was able, in a couple of hours, to gather a nice bag of pecans.

Sprung's Grocery sold Peters shotgun shells. They got 75¢ a box for them. They would also sell individual shells. Their price was 4¢ apiece for the individual shells. If memory serves, I was able to trade my bag of pecans for four shotgun shells.

Let me interject here that the first time I heard of posted land was after I was back from the service. When Mr. R. A. Drake chewed me out for squirrel hunting on his posted land, I told him that was the silliest thing I had ever heard. I said, "Man, I have hunted this place all of my life and you want to tell me I can't hunt here!"

Back to my shotgun shells. Sunday afternoon I went dove hunting. I knew Russell Cornelius had a patch of hegari on his place. I had seen a lot of doves on the power line that crossed the field of grain. When I arrived at the patch, I discovered that Russell had cut and bundled the hegari, for there were shocks of bundled hegari drying in the field. I arranged one of the shocks into a blind right in the middle of the field under the power line.

The doves obliged me by coming in droves and landing on the light line wire right over my head. There was one small problem.

Mrs. Bobby Wright, who had taught me in the third grade, had also introduced me to the joys of bird watching. Try as I might, I could not bring myself to shoot one of those beautiful birds. As I sat there in my blind, more and more doves flocked in to the hegari patch.

Before I stood up to leave I got to thinking how I would answer to "The Old Man" when I went home empty-handed. There was just no way that I was going to 'fess up to being too tender hearted to kill a mess of doves. I lined my new shotgun up on the largest concentration of birds on the wire. I touched off the round. Dead and dying birds rained down from the wire. I raced to the fallen birds. I jerked the heads off of any fluttering ones. Then I gathered the whole bunch up and headed home. My single, well-placed potshot had yielded enough doves for more than a big meal. The next time I went dove hunting I was able to kill a mess with much fewer twinges from a conscience built into me by Miss Bobby.

It was fried dove, cream gravy, and biscuits for supper that night. There was a real feeling of pride in me because I had furnished the meat. I puffed up like a toad when my brother-in-law asked me, "How many shells did you use to kill all these doves?"

Did not take me long to learn to ride up in the pasture on Ol' Skinflint and slowly herd a covey of quail into some thin cover. While they were concentrated there, I would dismount and make my shot. I could usually depend on a good mess of quail every time I made one of these potshots.

We leased a pasture that joined the back of our place. There was a small natural lake on that place. That winter I learned I could stay hidden beside Skinflint and walk him up into shooting range of the ducks feeding on the lake. I learned that I could softly whistle between my teeth and the ducks would gather up in a bunch to try to determine what made the noise. I made some unbelievable potshots on bunches of green wing teal and mallard [ducks] that winter. Even "The Old Man" got to asking me, "How many shells did you use to kill all those ducks?" Around my home a comment like that was pretty heady stuff.

As winter gave way to spring, I started squirrel hunting. Took me awhile to learn that squirrels would bunch up at breeding time. I also learned that baby squirrels would stay close together when they first came out of the nest. I did not waste many shells shooting at single squirrels. I had developed into a full-fledged potshooter.

Early in the winter when I was fourteen, Coach Schwarz, who was the high school coach, and Bascom Hays, who was superintendent of Edna schools, asked me to go duck hunting with them. I was so excited I could hardly sleep the Friday night before we went hunting on Saturday. We left before 5 A.M. and went to a rice field between Edna and Ganado.

Coach Schwarz took me and put me in some reeds at one end of a small lake. He took a position in some senabeans at the other end. The sun was just starting to rise when a nice flock of mallards came to the lake. They circled once, then came closer to circle again. Coach Schwarz hollered, "Take 'em." He stood up and dropped a pair with his double barrel.

I really did not understand what was happening. He had shot two times to kill two ducks. I thought he really must be lucky to hit even one of the flying ducks. He screamed at me, "Why didn't you shoot?" I told him that I was waiting for the ducks to land so I could kill a bunch of them.

Coach Schwarz chewed me out as only an old experienced football coach can chew. He impressed on me that a potshooter was one of the lowest forms of human life. That no real sportsman would ever shoot a sitting duck. That man totally destroyed me. I was humiliated. I had no idea that anyone ever shot at moving targets, much less on a regular basis. I had never been hunting with anyone with a gun to have seen it done.

I left Coach Schwarz and went to a huge rice stack between the lake and the car. I backed up on the south side of the stack to get out of the cold wind. I felt as low as a teenage boy can feel. I wallowed in my misery for a while and then I got mad. I made myself a promise that I was going to show that old son-of-a-bitch if it was the last thing I ever did. They picked me up in the middle of the morning. I had to put up with a good deal of teasing during the ride home. I added Mr. Hays to my get-even list along with Coach Schwarz.

I was working in Buddy Simon's grocery store on weekends and holidays. This gave me a regular income of $1.50 per week. I spent every cent I earned on shotgun shells. Every evening after school I would go up in the pasture after the milk cow. I took my shotgun with me along with a pocketful of shells. I shot at everything that moved. Cottontail rabbits, jack rabbits, doves, quail, meadow larks, hawks, killdeer, and plovers were all "hulled" on sight. I shot only at running or flying targets. In a short time I was able to hit one every once in a while. By the time winter, spring, and summer were over I could hit more than I missed. That fall I honed my skills on doves, quail, ducks, and geese. I made opportunities to hunt with other people. By the time winter was over, I thought I could shoot as well as any man with whom I had hunted.

The summer I was sixteen I got a job working at the ice plant. I received a man's wages of 40¢ per hour with time-and-a-half for overtime. Because of World War II, there were no new guns to be bought. One day I discovered a used shotgun for sale at Arnold's Hardware. It was a 16-gauge, Model 97 Winchester pump shotgun. It showed hard use, but it was solid as a rock. I bought it for $25.

When dove season came around, I started working on them with my Model 97. I quickly reached the point where I could smoke those birds coming or going, fast or slow, high or low. Then I started working on getting doubles and then even triples. There is no substitute for a driving, burning desire and young reflexes when it comes to mastering a shotgun.

Before October rolled around, I invited Mr. Hays and Coach Schwarz dove hunting. I lined us up on a fence line between a grain field and a small lake. We had a steady flow of doves either going to feed or to water. I poured the shot to those birds just as fast as I could. I missed few birds. In only a few minutes I had my limit. Among my birds were several that I had dropped while Coach Schwarz tried to get lined up for his shot. That rattled him a little, and he started off missing. When I stopped shooting, I harangued them both about their misses—more than a teenage boy should have. Coach Schwarz left and went to the lake to shoot. When it was time to quit, neither of them had a limit. Both had shot a bunch of shells.

Coach Schwarz walked up to me and laughed as he slapped me on the shoulder, which was about like being slapped by a grizzly bear. He said, "I. T, you keep working at it and you may learn to shoot that little old gun. Now put in your shirttail (his pet peeve) and let's go home."

Those words may have been as sweet a message as I ever heard. I had just been welcomed into the fraternity of sportsmen.

First Deer Hunt

There was a man who drove a team of two yokes of oxen. He came to Edna almost every August to gin a bale of cotton. His was the only team of oxen I have ever seen work. He lived at Speaks, Texas, and he told me that it took him two days to make the trip to Edna. The last time I saw him was in the summer of 1944. I visited with him for a while on the gin yard. In the course of this visit he gave me a piece of information that set me on fire. He said that he had seen a buck deer close to Speaks!

At that time deer were so scarce in the Coastal Bend portion of Texas that for me they just did not exist. I think hard times and hungry people had all but eliminated them. My interest in that deer sighting was not one of preservation of the species. Friend, I wanted to hunt and kill one.

Billy Paul was with me when I heard about the deer. We made each other a promise that during the Christmas holidays we would go to Speaks and kill that deer.

Billy Paul was a dandy hunting and fishing partner. He was physically tough and mentally there was just no way to discourage him. Bad conditions and hard luck were greeted by Billy Paul as if they were old friends. He had a smile ready for either of them. In camp he always took care of his share of the work. He was skilled with a knife, an ax, a .22 rifle, and a shotgun. Billy Paul and I caught a lot of fish together. Together we also killed our fair share of doves, quail, squirrels, ducks, and geese. Billy Paul was my friend.

As Christmas approached, we began to make plans for the hunt. Rifles were our first concern. Billy borrowed an old .30-40 Krag from his grandfather. His grandfather also gave him a big handful of ammunition to go with the rifle. We looked at the cartridges and the rifle, and we knew Billy was well armed for the hunt.

I knew Russell Cornelius had a deer rifle. It was a Model 92 Winchester in .44-40. I asked him if I could borrow his rifle. He never hesitated, just reached up to the rack over the door, and handed it to me. I fuddled around for a long time and finally asked him if I could borrow a bullet for the rifle. Because of World War II, there was no rifle ammunition for sale anywhere. Russell let me have all the ammunition he had, two fresh rounds and one that had been fired but had not gone off. Man! I was set.

Neither Billy nor I had ever fired a center-fire rifle, and we knew next to nothing about them. That did not stop us from having a number of arguments over whose rifle and cartridge made the best deer killer.

The rest of our gear consisted of a well-worn tarpaulin, a frying pan, an ax, a gasoline lantern, and some rope. For food I furnished a slab of cured bacon, some peanuts, and a small flour sack filled with sweet potatoes. Billy furnished a flour sack of biscuits and some Irish potatoes.

The day after school was out for the holidays, I rode my horse out to the Paul house. I had everything rolled up in two quilts and tied behind my saddle. It drizzled rain the whole way to his house. Billy had made arrangements for us to use his grandfather's 1936 Ford pickup truck. We rolled all our gear up in the tarpaulin and put it in the back of the truck. We left for Speaks in high spirits.

At that time all the rural roads I knew about in Texas were dirt roads. We found that the road that went to Speaks was in awful condition because of heavy rains. We spent the whole day with the truck either stuck in a mudhole or stuck in a ditch. When night fell we had traveled less than three miles.

We returned afoot to the Paul house to spend the night and the next morning we took a team of mules and pulled the truck back home. We decided that we would have to go on horseback as the roads were then in even worse condition because of the continuous rain and drizzle. We decided to take only our rifles, our bedding, the frying pan, the tarpaulin, and our food.

The next morning we left on horseback and still in high spirits. We rode at a steady pace with only a break for our noon meal. In the middle of the afternoon we came to a house. Since neither of us knew where Speaks was we stopped and asked at the house. The man who lived there told us we were at Speaks. We asked about the deer situation. His answer was that there might be a deer around there. I remember he made a big circle over his head with his arm and told us there might be a deer anywhere around there.

The drizzle stayed with us off and on all day. We decided to camp close to the Navidad River. About the time we chose a campsite, it began to rain hard. We made a lean-to out of the tarpaulin. We had hardly gotten the shelter up before a fresh norther blew in. We built a huge fire in front of the lean-to and tried to dry out our bedding. We unsaddled the horses and staked them out on some good Bermuda grass. Neither of us had brought a change of clothes, so we hung our clothes close to the fire to try to dry them out.

We were both cold and hungry. We fried up a big batch of bacon and Irish potatoes and started roasting a couple of sweet potatoes in the ashes. The hot meal warmed us a bit and also served to raise our spirits. We could tell that though the fresh norther was blowing with force, it was not lowering the temperature drastically. By the time we finished the fried potatoes and bacon, the rain had almost stopped and it was full dark.

We kept the fire blazing in an effort to dry our bedding, and we put back on our almost dry clothes. We sat and talked about our prospects for the coming day. We were both tired and getting sleepy. We raked the sweet potatoes out of the ashes and had a delightful snack before we turned in.

Since there was not one thing in our camp that would protect us from the wet ground, we just lay down on the ground close to the fire and went to sleep. We had to build the fire up several times that night to stay warm, but we both got enough sleep.

We were munching on fried bacon and fried biscuits well before dawn began to break. The rain had completely stopped and a few stars were showing. Billy had decided to hunt up in the higher ground completely out of the river bottom. My choice, for no good reason, was to hunt the river bottom. We had roasted some peanuts by the fire during the night, so we each took a pocket of peanuts and left hunting.

I covered a lot of ground that day. The wind was still strong out of the north. I did not see a living animal except a few birds all day long. We both returned to camp after dark.

We tended the horses and then cooked up a big supper for ourselves. We talked awhile but the warm campfire made us drowsy. We covered ourselves and went to sleep.

The next day was a repeat of the day before. The only difference was that the sky was completely clear and the wind had begun to slack off. We both saw rabbits and squirrels that day, but we only had our deer rifles and we would have starved before we wasted a bullet on small game. That night the wind laid completely, and it got pretty cold. I remember I added wood to the fire several times during the night.

As we started our third day of hunting, we stuck to our original plans. Billy to the high ground, me to the bottom land. The weather was perfect, clear blue sky, no wind at all and sharp, crisp temperatures.

I moved slowly, enjoying the day. An hour or so after I left camp I came to a grove of huge pecan trees. The heavy rains and high winds had caused most of that year's crop of nuts to fall. The ground was covered with pecans. I gathered up a pocketful and found a good seat up against a tree. I started cracking and eating pecans. They were wet from the rains, but they were sure good. I made no effort to be still or to keep from making noise. My interest was concentrated on eating pecans.

After a bit I caught a movement out of the corner of my eye. When I discovered it was a doe, I became so excited that I could hear my heart beat, the sound coming up my throat and out my open mouth. The doe was only about fifty yards from me. She was eating pecans too, shell and all.

Billy and I had never discussed anything about the killing of a doe. We both, I think, assumed that we would only see bucks. At that time I had no idea that there was a law concerning the killing of doe. I eased my rifle into my lap and slowly and quietly cocked the hammer. I sat there with indecision crawling around in my stomach like indigestion. To this day I cannot tell you what I would have done because at that moment a buck came out of the brush and started walking toward the doe.

I made myself sit still and wait. He reached a point where he was only thirty-five or forty yards from me. As I swung up the rifle, the deer turned toward my movement. He was facing directly at me. I swung and pointed the rifle just like I would have a shotgun. I never looked at the sights, just pointed and shot. At the shot that buck collapsed and never moved. He had been on higher ground than I was on, and I hit him low in the front of his chest right where I was looking at him. The bullet angled up and came out between his hips.

As I walked up to him, I was shaking so badly that I could hardly hold the rifle. When I saw that he was in fact dead, I lay the rifle down and walked around and around him. He was so beautiful that it almost took my breath away, and for a short moment I wished that I had not killed him. Then I reached down and examined his horns, a six pointer. I quickly lost my remorse at having killed him.

I got out my pocketknife and started dressing him. I had a terrible time with the bone and gristle as I opened the rib cage and an even worse time in the pelvic area. The bullet had passed through and made a huge mess of his whole digestive system. About the time I finished gutting him, I heard Billy whistle. I answered, and he came on in to me. When he saw my buck, he became as excited as I had been.

I tied all four legs together. Billy took the guns, and I hung my deer, body down, from my shoulder as we went to camp. My only thought was to get me and the buck home. We both realized the temperature was rising. The next day, we agreed, would probably be pretty warm. Too warm to keep the deer from spoiling.

We broke camp and made one bundle out of bedding, rifles, food, and tarpaulin. Billy tied it behind his saddle. I saddled my mare and started to load the deer behind my saddle, but she jumped as we went to lay the deer over her. A horn gouged her in the side. She dropped her head and threw a pitch fit. The deer flew high into the air and onto the ground. Those stirrups were popping over the mare's back with every jump. I finally caught her and calmed her down. Billy took his undershirt and blindfolded her. After a really rough struggle we got the deer loaded and tied down. I crawled up on her while Billy led her from horseback, still blindfolded.

He led her all the way to the house where we had asked the man for directions. We stopped and gave the man the fresh deer liver. We took off again with my mare still blindfolded and Billy with the lead rope snubbed up around his saddle horn. After a mile or so Billy took off the blindfold. The mare hopped around and snorted a bunch but that was all she could do because Billy had her head snubbed up high. After an hour or so we took off the lead rope, and I made it the rest of the way with no great difficulty.

It was after dark before we got to Billy's house. Mrs. Paul gave us cornbread and sweet milk. Best cornbread and sweet milk I have ever eaten. After the Pauls had looked my buck over, I headed on home.

The weight of the deer plus my weight made an unusual load for my mare. She was pretty tired, but she knew we were going home. I urged her into her good running walk and after a little more than an hour we were at the front gate at home.

Momma and Daddy were asleep. They got dressed to look at my buck. Daddy and I hung the deer from the limb of a hackberry tree. We skinned the deer by lantern light. Daddy thought it was cool enough to leave the deer hang overnight, but Momma instructed us to quarter it and bring it in so she could put it in the refrigerator.

A strange thing happened with my first deer. I got deer stomach and intestine juices all over me during the gutting process. I could smell my hands even as they hung at my side. The smell stayed on and with me all day long. I also had the deer rubbing against me all day as I rode in. As I skinned the deer, I got sick of the smell. Every time I went to eat a piece of that deer, the smell would come back to haunt me. I could not eat a bite of that deer. As a matter of fact, it was several years before I could eat and enjoy venison.

Daddy and I took the Pauls a hindquarter from my buck. I also gave Russell Cornelius some steaks, some ground meat, and a roast when I returned his rifle.

I sawed the horns off the deer skull. During the remainder of the Christmas holidays I blamed near wore those horns out showing them to everyone who would look at them.

Those horns are screwed to a board and hang on a wall in my private room today. They are the only deer horns I have saved from a lifetime spent hunting Those horns and that hunt are special. I have only to look at them and instantly I am flooded with a wave of sweet memories. That is one of the real joys of being an old hunter. One tends to forget the miserable conditions of past hunts, the rain, the cold, the wet bedding, the missed meals. As a matter of fact, the older I get the sweeter those past hunts become.

Maud

It was a beautiful Saturday in the fall of 1943. I had worked hard in the garden digging sweet potatoes all morning, and at noon Daddy told me I could go into town that afternoon. Though I did not know what excitement the afternoon in town would offer, I looked forward to it as a welcome relief from digging potatoes. I did know that one of the things I wanted to do was show off my almost new saddle, so I caught up my mare and left for town.

When I got to the courthouse square, I noticed a small group of people gathered between the road and the railroad track just east of the square. I knew there would be excitement in town, and sure enough that group of people was gathered around the constable who was auctioning off stray, unclaimed animals out of the city pound. The constable was selling a Jersey cow as I rode up. There were several bidders on the cow, but I had spent too many hours pulling and squeezing on the milking end of a Jersey cow to have much interest in her. However, the last animal left to be sold was a small, brownish black, mare mule, and she did interest me. I had tried for some time to work my saddle mare to a cart, but she was far too spirited an animal to accept such mundane labor. In my mind's eye I could already see that little mule pulling me in a cart.

After the Jersey cow sold, the constable led the mule up to the group of people. He asked for a bid on the mule. There were no bidders. He asked who would give five dollars for the mule. I could not believe my ears when no one took her. I had worked all summer at R B Department Store and had saved my money, so I had some money in my pocket. I told the constable that I would give the five dollars for the mule. His answer was that if I wanted to buy the mule he would have to have Daddy's approval of the sale. I went and got Daddy.

Kind of surprised me when I did not get the old, " A penny saved is a penny earned" lecture. He just told the constable that if I wanted the mule to sell her to me.

The constable let me have the grass rope the mule was tied with, so my mare and I took the mule in tow and headed home. I swung by Branch's barn to see if Albert Ware had any harness he could let me use, but Albert was not there. I also stopped by Russell Cornelius's place to see if he had any work harness. He told me he had sold his harness with his team. Not to worry I told myself, as I was confident I would find some way to solve the problem with the harness.

I put the mule in the barn and gave her a feeding of ear corn. She knew what to do with the corn. I clipped her mane and tail and trimmed her hoofs. It was a rough clip job, but she ended up looking pretty good. I judged her to be just under fourteen hands high and a little thin, weighing around six hundred pounds. I looked in her mouth, who knows? At least she was old enough to sleep by herself.

I started to go to the house, but I had this nagging question in the back of my mind. I got a spare bridle and found I had to let it out the whole way. My mule had a big head. I led her out in the pasture where no one could see me. I petted her back, no reaction. I slapped her back, no reaction. I leaned my weight on her back and she just stood there. I jumped up and balanced across her back on my belly. She did not even look around. I pulled my right leg over and sat up, still no reaction. I urged her forward and she took off in a brisk walk. I kicked her into a trot and found it to be as smooth as butter. I rode back to the barn and saddled her up with my almost new saddle. She acted as if she had been saddled every day of her life. I rode her all over the pasture and found no faults other than she did not rein as well as my saddle horse. Sure made me feel good about my five-dollar mule.

That night when Daddy came in he brought a collar, a collar pad, a pair of hames, two hames straps, two trace chains, a blind bridle, enough rope for reins, and a single tree, all shiny new. Thought for a while "The Old Man" had gone soft. No lecture on spending money on a mule and then a whole new set of harness to use on her.

I could hardly wait for Sunday afternoon. As soon after lunch as I could, I harnessed up the mule, crawled up on her back and headed for the Fenner boys' house. They had a cart, and using my new harness and a little of their rigging I soon had her hooked up to the cart. Sure felt good driving my five-dollar mule, who by this time had been named Maud, all over town. Had attracted the attention of several young maidens that afternoon. Convinced myself that there was nothing like a mule and the promise of a cart ride for getting one shy, backward boy off on the right foot with the ladies.

There was not much time during the next week after school and chores to pay much attention to Maud. I did slip her some corn each night though. Tuesday Daddy showed up with a one-horse moldboard breaking plow and a Georgia Stock (plow) with a bull tongue and a sweep. I began to get the idea that Daddy expected Maud to pull something other than a cart.

Saturday morning, after milking and during breakfast, Daddy told me to hook up Maud to the breaking plow and to flat break the orchard. I had watched teams plow, but I had never plowed myself. This was before the day of "on the job training," but in his own way Daddy explained to me that I was going to learn by doing.

Ol' Maud knew what she was doing, and after a bit I began to get the knack of it. Even began to sort of enjoy it. There was a deep sense of satisfaction in turning over the weed-fouled ground and leaving fresh plowed, pungent soil. As the morning hours went by, I discovered that I was working Maud harder than I was working and that she needed a breather every once in a while. At noon I gave Maud a little hay, a light feeding of corn, and a drink of water. By the middle of the afternoon we had finished breaking the whole orchard. To me it was a beautiful job. I have never felt better about a task completed for the rest of my life. Maud was real tired, but I was sure proud of her. I was kind of proud of myself too. I was a fifteen-year-old boy who that day felt like a man doing a man's work.

Daddy showed up with a big sack of turnip seed that night. He broadcast by hand turnip seed over the whole orchard. He told me that once the turnips were ready I could have all I could sell out of the patch—after I had thrown over the fence all the cattle wanted to eat. It was a perfect turnip fall—cool, wet, and no insects. I sold turnips to Sprung's Grocery and to Piggly Wiggly, all washed and tied up in bunches of five. At first they gave me twenty cents a bunch but later they reduced the price to a dime, then a nickel. Daddy never knew I sold almost $150 worth of turnips that fall and winter. Just to demonstrate the value of a dollar then, let me state that that was almost $50 more than the amount I earned working the months of June, July, and August at R B Department Store, six days a week, seventy hours per week.

As time went by, I learned how to bed up the flat-broke land using the moldboard plow so that it could be planted in rows. Breaking the land and bedding the land became easy. That moldboard plow would almost handle itself. However, after the vegetables such as peas, beans, corn, tomatoes, and okra were up, it was quite a different matter to use the Georgia Stock plow with a sweep and a bull tongue to control grass and weeds. Brute strength and mass worked best in controlling the Georgia Stock. Those were the two things I had in shortest supply. The Georgia Stock was easy on the mule and hard on me.

Several weekends each year some of my friends and I would go camping to hunt and fish on the Lavaca River. We would camp at a low-water bridge crossing. The public road is no longer open to that bridge as some group of well-meaning people have built a country club over it. We used Fenner's cart to haul food, cooking gear, and bedding to the river. There was always a hassle over whose horse would have to pull the cart. After I got Maud, that problem was solved because we could use her to pull the cart. She gave every appearance of enjoying the trip and would follow us with no one driving or leading her. In order to see what she would do, we raced our horses a mile or so ahead of her. She just struck a trot and kept on coming. From then on when we got out of town, we would just turn Maud aloose and go on to the river at any speed we wanted. She would bray and nicker a bunch if we ran off and left her, but we could depend on her to come on in to camp at a quick trot. I do not ever remember staking her out while we were camped, like we had to with the horses. I just turned her aloose. She never wandered off far from the horses.

When one is plowing, the natural place for the animal pulling the plow to walk is in the middle. This works fine when cultivating or breaking and bedding the land. However, if one wants to plow up and harvest a crop like sweet potatoes or peanuts, the animal pulling the plow needs to walk on top of the bed, and that is not the natural place for the animal to walk. Consequently the natural tendency is to wander off the top of the bed in order to walk in the middle. I found with Ol' Maud that anytime she wandered down into the middle when I wanted her on top of the bed, a light touch with a whip would get her and her attention back up on top of the bed. A correction or two in a day would generally be all that was required.

The army cut our fences and came on to our place in January of 1945. It was a group of antiaircraft personnel from the base at Palacios. They dug deep pits all over our place to put their antiaircraft guns. After a week or so they removed their guns and filled in their deep pits. Shortly after they left, it started raining and it rained a good one. Our cows would start to walk across one of those pits and bog down. They could not get out and if someone did not pull them out they would stay there until they died. Pulling cows from those pits was an odious, miserable, dirty, wet, chilling, backbreaking chore. The old cows would not cooperate in any way and were held by a seemingly unbreakable suction. The task of pulling cows was awarded to Maud and me. Sometimes in sheer frustration I would vent my anger over the situation on Maud but even at the time I was ashamed of myself because I realized Maud gave me her very best every time I asked for it. We finally had to move the cattle to another place in order to solve the problem.

I wanted to move my saddle pony and Maud when we moved the cattle but Daddy told me that they were too smart to walk off in a bog. The week after we moved the cows I was busy in school making up the work I had missed while I was getting the cattle out of the bogs. I did not pay any attention to my horse or mule. Saturday I did not see Maud, so I caught my mare and rode up in the pasture looking for her. I found her bogged down, and it looked like she had been there for a number of days. I went to the house and got a shovel, burlap bags, and a lot of rope. After a couple of hours and with the aid of my mare I had her out on firm ground. She could not get up. I tried to help her, but she still could not get up. When Daddy came in, I had him look at her. He got Russell Cornelius, and the three of us tried to get her up but with no success. I took her feed and water. She showed little interest in any of it.

Sunday afternoon Daddy told me that there was no hope for her, and that I should destroy her. I did not want to but sixteen-year-old boys did not argue with Daddy. I got my 16-gauge shotgun and made the long and horrible walk up to where she was. I talked to her for a while and explained the situation. I tried to shoot her in back of the head but it just did not seem the right way to do an old friend. I walked around and faced her and blew a hole in her head right between her eyes. It was instant death. I sat down and cried a little, then I got up, told her good-bye and went to the house to do the night chores.

I learned a lot from Ol' Maud. In my heart I think I made a better adult than I would have made because of her. I know that she gave me an interest in hard work, and that interest kept me out of a lot of teenage trouble.

Maud may have only been a five-dollar mule that no one wanted, but to me she was my friend, my helper, my companion, and my teacher. You know to this day, fifty years later, I still miss Ol' Maud.

Jack Blackwell

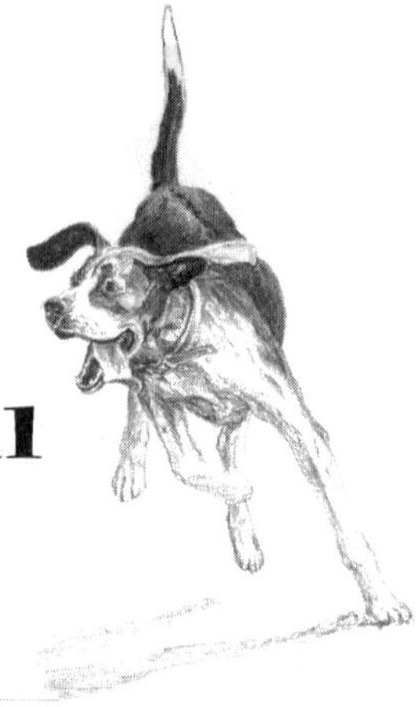

I have had few friends in this life who were as staunch and faithful as Jack Blackwell. He came to work for my Daddy early in the winter of 1940. The deal they made was that Jack got a good warm place to live and all the food from Momma's table he wanted. In return for a place to live and plenty of good food, Jack was to put in five and a half days' work each week. A day's work was considered to be ten or eleven hours. Daddy also gave Jack, from time to time, some of his old discarded clothes. Jack was a black man. He was 34 years old and worried about the national draft.

Jack and I hit it off from the start. We worked side by side on Saturday mornings and on school holidays like Thanksgiving and Christmas. My pay was about the same as Jack's. Only thing was I got a better deal on the clothes.

From the first Jack worked as steady as a man can work. He did good work, and if Daddy told him a different way to do a job, then that is the way the job was done. He built a bunch of fence that year and it was good fence.

One morning in the spring, after our planting had been done, Ol' Jack failed to show up for breakfast. He had said nothing to anyone. He just left. His leaving sure left me with a good supply of work to do.

Things rocked along until the next fall. One morning after it had begun getting cold, I started out the back door to do the morning milking, and much to my surprise, there was Jack sitting on the back steps. He told me to ask Momma if she would make him some cream gravy to go with her fine biscuits and bacon. I did not hear any of the conversation between Jack and Daddy, but it was as if Jack had never left. He just took right over with the work that needed doing. Only difference was Jack went to town on Wednesday afternoon. Seems that while Jack was gone he had been called up by the draft board. The army turned him down because he had syphilis. This fact was reported to the state health department, and Jack was required to take a syphilis treatment each week.

Jack carried out this pattern of showing up to work in the late fall and leaving in the spring for the whole time he was with us—four years. During hot weather, Jack drove a dump truck for Mr. Kanak, who was a road builder. Jack did love to drive a dump truck.

At this time of my life I had two dogs. One a cur dog named Trouble that ran loose. The other a potlicker hound named Speck that I kept at Branch's barn because my folks would not let me have a hound. Ol' Trouble was a pretty good varmint dog, and he treed quite a few possums. I did not take Trouble hunting, but I would sure wake up when I heard him treeing. I would go to the tree and get the possum and skin it out. Shoot man! A possum hide might bring as much as a dime. Jack started getting up and going to the tree with me when Trouble treed.

Was not long before Jack asked me if he could have the possum carcasses after I skinned them. I told him he was more than welcome to them. Jack then made a deal with Daddy to hold the live possums in a little chicken house we had and feed them corn until Saturday. After noon on Saturdays Jack and I would kill and skin the possums Trouble had treed during the week. This was seldom less than one or more than three possums. While I stretched my hides Jack would finish dressing the possum carcasses. He carried them to town and sold them, a nickel for a small possum, a dime for an average one and fifteen cents for the rare big one we caught.

Usually after we had caught a possum and put it in the chicken house, we would go to Jack's room over the garage and light his kerosene heater to warm up. We would talk in the soft light and warmth given off by the kerosene stove. At these times our conversations covered a range of topics. You know, real important subjects like dogs, guns, horses, fishing, and women. At these times Jack would usually roll a Prince Albert cigarette and smoke it. I had already developed the smoking habit before I ever met Jack, and when he would light up it would sure make me want a cigarette. I was afraid to ask Jack for a smoke because I knew if Daddy ever found out I was smoking he would punish me harshly. After a while though I developed enough trust in Jack to ask for a smoke.

One night, as we warmed up by the kerosene stove, Jack set a #3 washtub in front of me to catch the fallen grains of tobacco. He then proceeded to give me instruction in the fine art of rolling a good cigarette. It has been more than twenty-five years since I have smoked any kind of cigarette, but I would bet you a speckled pup that I can still roll a good tight cigarette.

Momma had a mystery going during the first months Jack worked for us. She had a large paring knife that she kept at a sink on our back porch. Momma would wash her garden vegetables at that sink and use the paring knife to trim or peel those vegetables. That knife would disappear on Saturday afternoons and then would reappear early Monday morning. When it turned up on Monday, it would be polished to a shine and razor sharp. Momma asked me if I had anything to do with the knife. For once I could joyfully and truthfully say, "Not me Momma!" Momma was never one to let a task started ever lay idle. In a short time I heard her ask Jack if he had anything to do with her disappearing knife. Jack looked down and mumbled "Yessum." Her next question was why he would take her knife without asking. Jack's answer was that he felt it necessary to have some sort of protection when he went to town and that he did not think she would mind. Momma's answer sure surprised me. Her answer was, "Jack, if you must use my knife, then ask before you take it."

Momma and Jack developed a special relationship. Jack would do almost anything if he thought it would please Momma. Momma on the other hand would cook special dishes just because Jack liked them. Jack was known to pull a joke on Momma. Like the time he planted her a row of cream peas before he left one spring. A cream pea is an almost white pea, but ever once in a while a black one turns up. When Momma started picking those cream peas that summer they turned out to be almost all black peas. That rascal, Jack, had picked out the black peas from a bunch of peas and planted them. When Momma got on him about the black peas his reply was that probably some of the black of his hand must have rubbed off on the peas as he planted them.

A couple of years after Jack started working for us, Daddy got a call from Sheriff Watson one Sunday morning. He stated that he had Jack locked up, and he wanted to know if Daddy wanted to come and get him. He said that Jack needed some medical attention. Seems that a couple of black men had tried to bully and abuse Jack at Moonglow Inn that Saturday night. The sheriff stated that both men had pulled knives and advanced toward Jack. Jack reached into his boot and pulled out Momma's paring knife. He fought his way into a corner and made a determined stand there. Sheriff Watson stated that when he arrived at the Moonglow Inn both attackers were down on the floor in pools of blood and that Jack was smoking a cigarette and cleaning Momma's paring knife with a paper napkin. Both of Jack's attackers recovered from their wounds, and no charges were ever filed. Daddy took Jack to Dr. Zipp to get his cuts sewed up. He had deep cuts on his forearms and a long slash across his right jaw. As bad as the cuts were, he went right to work Monday morning. I never did see that paring knife again. One day I asked Momma what happened to it. She told me she buried it in the garden.

I had two horses that I bought at the livestock auction ring, a bay horse I named Terrapin Bill, and a sorrel horse I named Skinflint. Both horses had a little age on them, and if memory serves I gave $5 for Bill and $7 for Skinflint. Ol' Skinflint could run a little, and I had great sport and success running him in races against my friends' horses. We had made a big corn crop that year, 1941 I think, on a place at Ganado. We filled the huge corn crib in our barn completely with ear corn and then stored the remainder in a shed by the hog pens. We fed the brood sows and the chickens and the milk cow with the corn from the shed.

I wanted to fatten up my two horses, so I fed them big feedings morning and night from the corn in the barn. In a four- or five-month period I made a pretty good hole in the ear corn stored in our barn. One evening Daddy came down to the barn as I milked our family milk cow, Ol' Lady, and looked around a little. As I started to the house with a bucket of milk, I saw Daddy talking to Jack at the hog pens. I heard Daddy in a harsh cold voice ask Jack what he had done with the missing corn. Daddy demanded to know if he had sold it and to whom he had sold it. Jack stood straight and tall under Daddy's assault. I heard him answer that he had never taken an ear of corn in his life.

At Edna, Texas, in the early 1940s, a black man had few rights. It was an everyday fact of life that if a white man accused a black man of theft, then that black man was as good as convicted and would serve jail time. Jack was simply too loyal for his own good. I knew he knew I had fed that corn to my horses, but I realized he would never reveal that fact to anyone—ever.

I am pretty sure in a ten-minute period in the late winter of 1941-1942 at the ripe old age of fourteen, I developed my first stomach ulcer. I had also developed a bad case of hyperventilation and rapid heart beat to go along with a dry mouth and a throat that would not swallow.

Momma called us to supper just after I got the milk to the house. I knew Jack could hear our conversation at the kitchen table as he ate at his little table on the back porch. I can still in my mind see Daddy at the table with a harsh, grim set to his face. I could not swallow a bite of food. I realized the earth was not going to open up and suck me away from my situation, no matter how badly I wanted it to happen. I reached down and got a hold of the little courage I had left in me. I confessed that I had fed all the missing corn to my horses. Daddy's wrath spilled over on me like boiling water, but you know I felt pretty good knowing Jack was out of his troubles.

Old Trouble treed that night. Jack met me at the tree. We went up to his room after we got the possum. Jack rolled a cigarette and handed the can of Prince Albert tobacco to me. I rolled a cigarette and handed the can back. "Jack," I said, "I am sorry." Jack answered, "Ah, that's all right."

Jack did not show up at our house in the fall of 1944. When December came around and he had still not shown up, Daddy asked Sheriff Watson to find out what happened to him. A few weeks later Sheriff Watson told Daddy that Jack was in Beaumont, Texas, married to a rich widow and driving his own dump truck. Hot damn! I was proud of Jack.

I never saw Jack or heard of him again. I know I owe him a huge debt. There is no doubt in my mind that I developed into a better person because of my association with him. I give him credit for starting me thinking that a man's color had little bearing on his intelligence, his integrity, his courage, or his loyalty. Jack Blackwell was a good man. Jack Blackwell was my friend.

Speck

My first dog was a cur whose appearance showed a dominance of German shepherd. He was my inseparable companion and we shared all things, good and bad. I remember once that he and I had slipped off to some mule barns that were several blocks from our house in Ganado, Texas. I was about five years old, and I had a good slingshot. There were quite a few cottontail rabbits around those barns, and he and I were trying to get one. When we returned home, Momma broke a limb off a peach tree to give me a switching for slipping off to hunt. When she raised the switch to strike me, my cur-dog growled at her and bared his teeth. She went in the house and got Daddy, who came out and thrashed the dog, while Momma switched me.

I remember, when he was only a clumsy pup and I was five, that I stepped on a board with three rusty nails sticking through it. The nails extended out at least two inches from the board and I jobbed them in to the hilt. Daddy had to lay me down, put his foot on my leg and jerk the nails out. To this day I use that experience to determine how badly something hurts me. I was given the standard treatment of the day for such an injury: My foot was soaked in coal oil (kerosene). The next day my foot was swollen and discolored, so Momma and Daddy decided that it should be soaked in Epsom salts and hot water. Momma then decided that salt pork should be put on the foot so that the nail holes would stay soft and drain. Well, my pup and I shared that salt pork. Momma would tie a piece on my foot. The pup would slip around and eat it. There is no way for me to know which did the job, but I must say that either the coal oil, the Epsom salts, the salt pork, the dog licking, or a combination of these had my foot well enough in about a week so that I could hobble down to the barn to get ear corn to feed the hog.

Speck

After we moved to Edna, my first dog became a nuisance in town and was given away. I was not consulted about this. I just came home from school one day and the dog was gone.

There was a vacant lot next to our house in Edna. We would stake Ol' Bossy, the family milk cow, to graze on this lot. Across the road from this vacant lot was the home of a family named Sterling. Mr. Sterling worked at Westhoff Mercantile. I had the impression that he was the manager or bookkeeper, but I really do not know what his responsibilities were. I do know that he and I got along just fine.

Mr. Sterling and I once made a deal wherein I kept a horde of jackdaws from building nests in an oak tree beside his house. For this service he furnished me almost all the ammunition I wanted to shoot in my BB gun. The persistence of those jackdaws convinced me at an early age that the meek would not inherit the earth but that the coyotes, the hawks, and the yellow jackets would be here long after the rabbits, the doves, and the butterflies were gone.

Mr. Sterling had a pen full of dogs close to his house. I asked him why he kept them. His answer was that they were Walker hounds used mostly to run wolves. He told me a little about how they were hunted. I had a compelling interest in his hounds, and I asked him question after question about them. He shocked me when he commented that if I was so interested in hounds, why not go hunting with him? My heart felt as if it had stopped beating and without another word I left running to the house to get Momma's permission. My joy at the idea of getting to run hounds was a short-lived one because Momma said that running hounds was not for me. She stated that all hound men did was go out, build a fire, turn the dogs aloose, and then drink whiskey all night. She said that she had brothers who hunted, and that she understood about such things.

Beginning with that night I started a long-range program designed to get Momma to change her mind. I did this knowing full well that Momma was a woman with a never-bending sense of right and wrong. I also knew from experience that Momma's no meant no.

I am pretty sure that Mr. Sterling talked to my mother about me going hunting with him. I think he convinced her that he would be the keeper of my morals while I hunted with him. The year was 1939, I was eleven and Momma had given me permission to go hunting with Mr. Sterling. I made myself a promise that fall day, a promise that I would never mix hunting and drinking. It has not been a hard promise to keep.

The night we went hunting was a cool, clear night, probably in September. I remember that we went somewhere in the vicinity of Louise, Texas. We hunted from a dirt road in some pretty heavy timber country. The first thing we did was build a small campfire. Then Mr. Sterling cast an old bitch. After a wait of ten or fifteen minutes we heard her strike. Her first long bawl produced goose-bumps on the back of my neck. She bawled a few more times, and then her mouth changed to a chop. It was a beautiful running chop, and it made the timber echo. Mr. Sterling explained that when she changed mouth she had jumped the fox. He turned another hound to her, and when that hound had harked in to the line he would turn loose another. In short order he had all five hounds running in a pack as they drove the fox.

It was a beautiful race, and the fox never took the hounds out of our hearing. There were times when the pack drove at a torrid pace, making the woods tremble with their roar. This would be punctuated with moments of silence, when the fox played some trick on the dogs. Then some hound would find the lost trail, and the race would be on again. Mr. Sterling described what was happening the whole time, and he helped me pick out individual hounds by their mouths in the pack. To be honest with you, I felt I knew what was happening without an explanation.

I have no idea how long the race lasted, but eventually the sound of the pack completely changed. Only a couple of the hounds were giving mouth. Mr. Sterling said that the fox had gone up a tree and that the hounds were treeing him. We went to the tree, which was not too far from the truck. With the aid of a flashlight he showed me the gray fox. He then called the dogs from the tree, and we started back to camp. He impressed on me that the fox was saved to be run another day. He also stated that his hounds were coyote hounds, wolfhounds as he called them, and that they were better at running a coyote than they were at running a fox.

Before we got back to camp, another pack came in hearing. Our pack left us, harking into the new pack. Mr. Sterling recognized the hounds in the new pack, and he said that we would move to their owner's camp to listen to the race. This second race lasted a long time and ended in a loss. That was the end of the hunt, but it took until daylight for all the hounds to home back in. Mr. Sterling's hounds homed back to our first fire.

One of the men I had hunted with that night was a Mr. Gillespie. A short time after that hunt we moved to the country. I was in town one day when I saw Mr. Gillespie. He asked me how I liked running hounds, and I told him that someday I would have my own pack. He said that if that was my feeling, then I could have a pup one of his bitches had under his barn. A check at home cut short my feeling of good fortune because Momma said she would not tolerate a hound pup on the place.

I had a dear friend. He was a black man who hand milked the dairy cows for our neighbor, Claudius Branch. Albert Ware was a kind, patient man who was never too tired or busy to listen to the problems of a budding white adolescent. Just as soon as I could, I sought out Albert to pour out my pup problem to him. Well Albert had a solution for my problem. He said that if I got the pup, he would keep him for me at the Branch's barn. He would feed the pup milk. I was to furnish the solid portion of its diet, cornbread. It was a most difficult task slipping enough scraps and cornbread out of the house to supplement the milk Albert furnished.

The pup showed to be mostly bluetick. Albert named him Speck. He developed into a small-sized hound. He had hound ears, gave bawl mouth on a trail, and would bark up enough to be called a tree dog. He was pure potlicker. I never hunted him anywhere but on Dry Creek, which ran across our place. He ran and caught or treed dozens of possums. He bayed more than a few skunks. He would tree squirrels, and in the three or so years I ran him he treed three coons. Just so you understand, those were the only three coons that made tracks on Dry Creek during that time.

Speck may not have been a very good coonhound, but he and I made up with persistence what we lacked in talent. During fur season I got the hides of all the animals caught and skinned. Albert and Jack Blackwell, the black man who lived on our place part of the time, took the carcasses. Skunk hides were worth about a nickel, possum hides up to a dime, and I am pretty sure I received about fifty cents for coon hides. Albert and Jack got from a nickel to a dime for possum carcasses, and I think Albert kept all the coons to eat himself.

Ol' Speck would show his raw courage when he bayed a skunk. The sequence of events would run something like this: Speck would bay the skunk and stop his attempts to escape. Then he would charge in, making an effort to catch and kill the skunk. The skunk would hit him directly in the face with a well-aimed stream of skunk scent. This would stop Speck, and he would become deathly sick, throwing up everything in his stomach. Speck would then go in and bay the skunk again—repeating the whole process time after time. Eventually, usually the fifth or sixth time, the skunk would run out of scent and Speck would have his way with the skunk. Most dogs would give up after the first squirt, but not Ol' Speck.

Skunk scent is a most persistent odor. A human body, when exposed to skunk scent, will keep smelling like a skunk for days. Clothing will hold the scent for an even longer period of time. After Speck killed his skunk, my job of skinning the skunk began. To me that was not too bad a job because I sort of like the smell of skunk. My problem was that I could not go home with the skunk scent on me. The solution to this problem came from my mother who once mentioned that tomatoes would neutralize skunk scent. With this bit of information I set about stealing Momma's home-canned tomatoes and hiding them in the barn.

When Speck caught a skunk, I would strip off all my clothes, shoes and socks included. Then I would skin the skunk, wash myself with canned tomatoes and rinse off either in the creek or a cow trough. Be aware that skunks were only skinned in the coldest of cold weather when their fur would be the thickest. Makes me cold to this day to think about undressing in the dead of night to skin a skunk, so I could bathe with tomato juice, so I could rinse off in a cow trough. All this was done in order to get a nickel for a skunk hide. Just so you know, the nickel was not all that important to me, but Speck catching the skunk was. I skinned those skunks because I felt I would have let Speck down if I did not hold up my end of our partnership.

In order to have time to run Speck, I would make excuses for reasons that required me to be in town at night. Studying with a friend, special band practice, or a meeting of a school club were excuses regularly used. On weekends going to a movie, going to a party, going to a community teenage dance, or going to church were some of the excuses I used to go hunting. I can remember Daddy chewing me out a number of times for staying out so late at a dance, when in fact I was on our place the whole time hunting varmints.

I had an unquenchable drive to run a hound, and I was willing to pay any price to fulfill that desire. My conscience quickly adjusted to lying about my whereabouts or stealing scraps for Speck .

Albert died, as I remember in February of 1945, and Claudius Branch was in the navy by this time. I volunteered to milk Mrs. Branch's cows until she was able to sell them at the end of May. Speck got sick during this time. I talked to Mr. Sterling about him, but the worm pill he furnished seemed to make him worse. He just quit eating and slowly life seeped out of him. My efforts went to naught, and Speck died.

Hunting Speck on varmints fed a need within me that was as real as my need for food or water or air. I felt compelled to run my hound. Speck was a real ego builder for one shy, insecure, teenage boy. My schoolmates would gather around and be impressed by my tales of our accomplishments, some real, some imagined. After I caught a boar coon, Albert showed me how to remove and clean the bone in its penis in order to make a toothpick. I would proudly stand on the schoolyard and pick my teeth with it. The status that toothpick gave me, since no one else had one or could get one, made it my most valuable possession.

I left home in the summer of 1945. I left with big holes in my social development. I had not developed any skills at all in mingling with girls my age. To this day I have never learned to dance. I was fifty years old before I was halfway comfortable at a party made up of men and women. But more important to me, I knew how to run the varmints out of the woods with a sorry potlicker hound. I could use a shotgun as if it were a natural extension of my body, and given a string and a fishhook or a gig and a lantern I could produce catfish out of the Navidad and Lavaca Rivers on command.

Shoot man! I thought I was ready for the world.

Pluma

Pluma was a good honest wolfhound. He always did his best to help the pack run a coyote, and he seldom did anything to hurt the race. He was not a great hound, but any hound that was better than Pluma was a real good one. Some idiot of a landowner shot Pluma one morning as he was homing back after a night's race to the spot he had been cast from to hunt. The bullet blew a hole in Pluma's neck. The wound never healed over and consequently left a direct passage from the outside into his throat. He could breathe through this hole and when he ate some of his food would dribble out of the hole. I am not maintaining that he was an appetizing dog, only that he was a good honest hound. He belonged to Alvin Day.

I moved to San Marcos, Texas, in 1949. I fell in with a bad crowd shortly after I moved. Alvin Day, Perry Lee Gary, Corrie Smith, Jody Dupree, Hop Jackson, and a few other citizens of San Marcos ran coyotes with hounds. I just sort of naturally took up with this group. I had run my own hounds for almost ten years before I met these hunters, but my hounds had been potlicker varmint dogs that ran anything that walked, wiggled, or crawled. At the time I met the San Marcos wolf hunters, I was like a genetic alcoholic who had never had a drink. I was a born wolf hunter. I just had never been on a wolf hunt. Alvin Day and Perry Gary took care of that blind spot in my education on a Saturday night in the fall of 1950. They took me hunting to an area southeast of Devine, Texas.

Alvin and Perry enjoyed hunting as much as any two hunters who ever went to the woods with a hound. I have seen a lot of hunters who had a good time when everything was going right, but Alvin and Perry always seemed to have a good time even when everything went bad. A portion of their fun was derived from the jokes they would play on hunting companions and each other. At times these pranks would be spontaneous responses to a situation, while at other times they would be long-range, well-thought-out, plans of action. Only once did I ever see one of their pranks backfire on them.

My first hunt in South Texas revealed that part of the world to be a harsh, cruel, beautiful country. That one hunt got me involved with rattlesnakes, one of which was fully as long as I am tall; with spiders that are as large as my open hand; with wasps that fed on the tarantula spiders; with thousands of acres of vegetation, each species of which appeared to be blessed with thorns; with clouds of mosquitoes that would magically appear from nowhere; and with a herd of javelina that cut up one of the hounds to the point that he died the next day. That first hunt also introduced me to one of my heroes, the little South Texas coyote.

Perry and Alvin were quick to discern that the wounds inflected on Ol' Traveler had really impressed me. Thereafter each time one of them saw me he would entertain me with tales, real or imagined, that demonstrated the fierceness of the South Texas javelina. After a time their tales had the desired effect, and I think an apt description would be that I had become javelina shy. I was sure ripe for a javelina prank.

The next time I went hunting with them, they poured out javelina stories all the way down to the Campbell Ranch, which is close to the town of Campbellton. When we got there, we built a fire, made coffee, and sat back and enjoyed cups of the fresh brew. Before long a family of coyotes began to bark and howl a half-mile or so north of camp. Alvin suggested that he and I walk the hounds toward those coyotes. Perry told me later that Alvin planned to play a javelina prank on me. He planned to recount lurid tales of javelina assaults as we walked to the coyotes, and at an appropriate moment he would goose me from behind as he made grunting sounds.

Long before we reached the spot where the coyotes had cackled, we walked into a herd of javelina rooting in prickly pear cactus. I remember that moment as containing more animal activity than I have ever witnessed before or since. Mixed dogs and javelinas running in every direction. Dogs baying, barking, yelping, scared or hurt. Javelinas squealing, snorting, and popping teeth.

When the activity calmed down, I realized that I was up in a good-sized mesquite tree. Alvin was up in another. We were in the middle of a dead quiet. After a bit, Alvin suggested I get down out of my tree. I declined the offer, but I remembered my manners and returned his invitation. He too declined. After a long empty silence, Alvin suggested that we climb out of our trees at the same time. Several false starts later, and we were both on the ground. Nothing but stark silence greeted us. We walked to each other and started to walk back to camp. My flashlight showed a good deal of white around Alvin's eyes. I do not know what his flashlight showed. We had only taken a few steps when we heard a javelina pop his teeth behind us. I beat Alvin to the closest tree and started up. Alvin, in his wild effort to climb, pulled me down while climbing over my back. In my panicked state I fought at the tree and Alvin to the point that we both ended up in a pile on the ground. Our next effort finally got our badly battered bodies up in the tree. Alvin had his flashlight in his pocket, I never did find mine. Alvin turned on his light and surveyed the situation. All the light revealed was Ol' Pluma standing there wagging his tail. While still in the tree, we deduced that Pluma had been lying down behind some cactus. When we got down from the tree to leave, he jumped up to join us. As he jumped up he sucked air through the hole in his throat, making the sound of a javelina popping his teeth.

In the thirty-five years since that night I have never heard Alvin mention a javelina again. You might say that Alvin is a little javelina shy himself. Alvin had open-heart surgery awhile back. He may not know. I am sure his doctor does not know. It just so happens though that I think I know the exact moment his heart problems started. You might say his heart was damaged from the fright caused by a good honest hound with a hole in his guzzle . . . Ol' Pluma.

High Pockets

High Pockets was a beautiful little lemon and white Walker bitch. At first glance one got the impression that she would be an extremely fast hound. Looks were misleading, though, because in a pack of wolfhounds she was only another member of the pack and could usually be found running toward the back of the pack. The first time I saw her was in the fall of 1951. She was tied in the back of Corrie Smith's truck. She looked to be about a year old. We had been hunting in South Texas, and Corrie had picked her up as she crossed a road. The pack had crossed ahead of her, and Corrie was not all pleased with her because she was running behind. I made a comment that she sure was a pretty thing, and Corrie told me to put my collar on her and take her. He said that she was not fast enough for him to keep. I took her. When I got home, Billye took one look at her and named her High Pockets. I liked that name because it fit her looks, and according to Corrie, her pedigree went back to the famous Walker hound, Hi Doctor.

I ran High Pockets all of that winter on coyotes, in packs made up of combinations of hounds belonging to my hunting friends like Alvin Day, Perry Lee Gary, Corrie Smith, Jody Dupree, and Hop Jackson. She was run often enough and long enough to demonstrate that she was a game hound, but she never distinguished herself in any way during that winter.

One night in February of 1952, I could not find a single hunter who wanted to run dogs. Since I only had two hounds, Rough and High Pockets, I decided to go and run a fox. I had never run Rough on fox, but he had already made a name for himself as an extremely fast, hard driving, wolfhound. In fact, he was considered an outstanding hound by all who heard him run. I took my two dogs to an area close to the community of Red Rock. I came to a place where the road made a Y. It looked like good country to me, so I stopped, cast my hounds, built a fire, and put on a pot of coffee. Before the coffee was finished, the dogs struck and the race was on.

I could not understand what was happening because High Pockets was running steady giving plenty of clear chop mouth, while Rough was only running in a hit and miss fashion. He would be in the race for a bit giving his beautiful horn mouth. Then I would not hear him again for quite some time. Curiosity got the best of me, so I proceeded to have a look as best I could. It was a moonlit night and even though I did not have a flashlight, I struck out to the running dogs. I was able to get right up on top of them quite a number of times in the next half of an hour. What I saw was a revelation. Ol' Rough would hit the track and take it away from High Pockets. He would drive on the line until the fox changed directions. At that point Rough would drive on for quite a long overrun. In the meantime High Pockets would continue with her work, and, when she got to the spot the fox changed directions, she would turn with him with hardly a falter. That left Rough having to gather himself and hark into High Pockets. As I started back to the fire, High Pockets changed her mouth. I suddenly realized that little bitch was barking treed. I went to the tree but without a light I could not find the fox. I caught the dogs and went home.

I had heard hunters say Streak, who belonged to Ben Marks, was a good foxhound. He was a beautiful ring-necked Trigg. Experience had shown me that he sure was not a wolfhound because under the pressure of a hard-driving pack he would quit and come in. The next night I left Rough at home, and I borrowed Streak to run. This time I took a flashlight. I cast High Pockets and Streak at the same spot I had hunted the previous night. They struck in a short time. They sounded as if they were running while tied together. It was a beautiful race with High Pocket's clear bell chop and Streak's high pitched "pewing" squall. When that fox went up, I found that Streak was a dandy tree dog. I caught them at the tree and went home.

Jody Dupree had a hound named White Man. He was a good hound, but he had gotten old and a little slow in our wolf packs. The next time I went hunting, I took White Man along with High

Pockets and Streak. Those three hounds gave me the impression that they were made to run together. They were a beautiful combination of ability, working speed, and mouth. White Man, by the way, had a big coarse chop mouth to go with High Pocket's bell chop and Streak's high squall. They ran the track in such a steady manner that our little gray foxes could seldom stay ahead of them longer than thirty minutes. White Man would not tree, but he would stay at a tree with a tree dog. High Pockets, by herself, would only hold a tree for a few minutes. Ol' Streak would usually hold a tree for fifteen or twenty minutes, which was ample time for me to get to most trees. There was not another hound in my hunting area that could be added to these three hounds without hurting the pack effort.

This was my first trip past the concept of the hard-driving individual hound, as opposed to the team effort of a pack hound. I quickly learned a good pack hound was a lot harder to come by than one that was considered outstanding because of his speed and drive. To this day my favorite-sized pack to run on any animal is a three-dog pack. A good three-dog pack demands that each hound must be capable of running the animal by himself and that each member of the pack will unselfishly give his talents to the pack effort.

These three hounds made the best pack of foxhounds I have ever listened to. I ran them together for about six months. Streak was known as a quitter in a wolf pack, but he never failed to hunt and run in this little fox pack. I developed a pattern wherein I would take the three out and cast them. Usually by the time I could make coffee and drink a cup they would have one going. They seldom failed to tree the fox, and when possible I would go to the tree. I would praise them and then lead them from the tree. I never jumped a treed fox out for them because I wanted to preserve my foxes. I would cast them again, and most of the time they would start another fox. If they treed this second fox and I could get to the tree, I would lead them off and recast them. I would then go back to camp and crawl in my bedroll and go to sleep.

Many times I remember waking up because they were running another fox. I would listen until I would drift off into sleep again. At daylight I would wake up. With no exceptions when I woke up, White Man would be curled up on the left side of my bedroll. Streak would be on the right side and High Pockets would be at my feet. I would heat up the coffee, have a cup, load up, and head home. I do not remember ever having to look for one of them or ever having to call one in with my blowing horn. A pack that handles itself is a luxury that I have not enjoyed either before or since.

In the fall of 1952 Streak died in Corrie Smith's dog pen. Then a couple of months later White Man failed to come in after a race in South Texas. He was probably the victim of a snakebite or a coyote trap. High Pockets was stolen out of a race in the Campbellton area. Months later, strictly by chance, I saw her in a pen of hounds belonging to a bobcat hunter from Devine. The cat hunter was a decent sort of fellow, and, after I explained to him that I would kill him where he stood if he lied to me, he told me that he had bought the bitch in good faith from a man who lived close to Seguin. I took my dog. I went to the Seguin man's house and settled my account with him. Some months later the cat hunter came to me and asked to buy High Pockets.

He offered me a fair price, $35 as I remember, and I sold her to him. I sold her because I was not able to find another hound matched to run with her after Streak and White Man died.

A young man's dreams are made of the things he wants to do. An old man's dreams are about the things he has done. Times change and values change, but in 1952, I could have had Streak for the asking and I could have bought White Man for less than $40. I would then have owned the best pack of foxhounds I ever heard at a cost of less than $40. Today a pack with the ability of those three hounds would cost considerably more than a thousand dollars. The saddest part is that today I would be hard pressed to find enough country in the whole of Central Texas to run such a pack of foxhounds.

The beauty of being an old hunter is that I can sit here and remember back to those times. I can almost get the feeling of being alone and hunting in good open country. I can almost smell the campfire. I can almost taste the good fresh camp coffee. I can feel the chill of a frosty night. I can almost even hear that splendid three-dog pack come into hearing, driving the fox ahead of them. It borders on being better than the actual hunting because in my Old Man's dreams that wonderful little pack never makes a mistake and they always tree the fox.

Damn, but it is good to be alive and born a hunter. It is good to have been able to hunt in better times. I truly feel sorry for those of you who missed the opportunity.

Five Dollars to Boot

I was really worried. Ol' Rough had been lost for over a week. He was my best coyote hound, and there was no way I could replace him.

Rough came into my possession in a rather roundabout manner in the spring of 1951. You see, Alvin Day maintained that Slim Northington owed him some money. Slim did not honor this claim. Slim owned Rough, but for all practical purposes he had quit running hounds. I wanted a good hound, but I had no money to buy one. So, Alvin told me to buy Rough from Slim and to ask for a ten-day trial before I paid for him. I did as instructed, and after a great deal of haggling Slim and I agreed on a price of $35 for Rough. Alvin told me, at the end of the ten-day trial, to write Slim and tell him that I had left the money at Alvin's store and for Slim to pick it up there. I mailed this letter as I left for an extended hunt in South Texas. Alvin told me that Slim came by for his money and Alvin told him that it had been applied against the debt. My understanding was that some rather harsh words were exchanged before Slim left. Be that as it may, Slim never mentioned the sale of Rough to me after that. I paid Alvin the $35, at a rate of $5 per month.

Rough was a pretty good wolf dog. He was a Goodman hound and stood twenty-eight inches at the shoulder. He was the largest hound I have ever seen. He had an outstanding horn mouth that could easily be identified no matter the size of the pack in which he ran. He was a hard-driving hound and could be found on the front end of any pack. I used Rough as a strike dog because he hunted well, would go to a barking wolf and would not take off after game like deer or jack rabbits. I ran Rough about two years. In that time I was never ashamed of him. He was an honest hound in all of his work. He had two major faults. First, he would not put his mouth on a coyote after he had run it down, and, second, because of his size and his style of hard running he could only run well about two times a week. He would always be a badly battered hound for at least two days after a hard race.

Corrie Smith came by my house while Rough was lost and asked me to go hunting with him. Since he planned to hunt in the general area where Rough was lost, I agreed to go with him. My hope was that Rough would hark into Corrie's pack. I started to change into some warmer hunting clothes, but Corrie told me not to bother as we would only make a short hunt, since he had a hard day planned for the next day. I grabbed a light jacket. Corrie had on a new pair of dress pants, a new shirt, and new dress shoes. He also had a light jacket. I loaded my bitches, High Pockets and Roxie, in with Corrie's pack, and we left.

We went to a spot between Dean's Store and Kingsbury to cast. It was a beautiful night in January. The day had been pretty warm with no wind and lots of sunshine. When the sun went down, radiation cooling soon had the temperature plummeting down. We must have turned out on top of a coyote because the strike dogs almost instantly opened. Immediately we turned the whole pack to them, and they left going northeast. After a while they went out of hearing, so we followed them in Corrie's truck, going up a gravel road. We stopped several times, but each time the hounds were still farther to the northeast. We were miles from where we cast when we caught up to the hounds. They had changed directions and were driving to the west.

We jumped into Corrie's truck to follow, but Corrie could not get it in gear. As we worked trying to get the transmission to work, the pack went out of hearing. Corrie had me try to operate the gearshift lever while he fuddled under the hood. He hollered for me to try harder. I did. He shouted for me to quit fooling around and apply more pressure. I did. He screamed at me to really bear down on the shift lever. I did. The gearshift column sheared in two from the pressure I put on it. The two of us lacked the mechanical understanding of a freshly weaned monkey, but we both understood his truck would go no farther that night.

As we built a fire in the middle of the road to ward off the ever-cooling temperature, Corrie speculated that someone would come by and give us a ride. No one did. The night got colder. The fire got larger. That was the beginning of our problems. We were cold and the only wood available was dead, insect riddled, mesquite. It burned well, but it would quickly burn to ashes. There was another problem. That whole country was infested with grass burs. When I touched the end of my index finger down in the middle of the road, I got five grass burs in the end of that one finger. Corrie tried to lie down. The grass burs cut short that idea. So there we were—no transportation, no hounds, plenty of grass burs, and lots of cold.

Finally, Corrie pulled the seat out of his truck and dragged it up to the fire. Under the seat he found an empty burlap bag. He tossed it to me. He stretched out beside the fire on the truck seat. I stretched out on the burlap bag and the grass burs. Corrie was soon asleep. The fire burned down. In his sleep Corrie drew closer to the warmth of the coals and ashes. In fact, he got so close it charred the whole back of the legs of his new dress pants. From time to time one of us would build up the fire. Some time after midnight the temperature fell below freezing. We were not comfortable.

A couple of hours before daylight Corrie kicked me awake and said we would walk down the road to a black man's house. There he assured me, we would get a ride to where he lived over his tavern, the Be Back Inn. He said his wife would prepare us a good breakfast before we went into town to get Alvin Day's truck to tow his truck in for repairs.

We started walking. After a mile or so Corrie was hobbling from pain from blisters caused by his new shoes. As we kept on, mile after mile, Corrie continued to remind me how good his wife's breakfast was going to taste. Finally, about daybreak, we arrived at the black man's house. My initial impression was that the black man was not particularly happy with us for showing up on his door-step at daybreak. In fact, the black man was less than enthusiastic about the prospect of having to haul two rednecks some twenty miles on that cold morning. I saw Corrie slip the black man some money and I heard him promise more when we were delivered to Be

Back Inn. Really goes to show you that snap judgments are not to be trusted. Why actually that was a right friendly black man.

We got to Be Back Inn. Corrie settled with our new friend. We walked up the stairs and Corrie unlocked the door. Inside, Mrs. Smith was still in bed asleep. Corrie woke her up and gave her the good news that she would get to prepare us some breakfast. When Corrie turned to leave the room, Mrs. Smith spied his burned pants. She reminded Corrie that they were new pants and that she had asked him to change pants before he left to go hunting. Corrie reached down to show her that the pants were not really badly burned. The material crumbled to his touch leaving a big bare V extending from the knee down to the cuff. Mrs. Smith was by this time fully awake. From her words I began to get the idea that she questioned his mental capacity. I think I even heard her refer to him as one of the long-eared variety of barnyard animals.

Corrie took me by the arm, and we backed out of the apartment. He said that he had decided to eat at a cafe in town. As we got into Mrs. Smith's new Packard, she shouted down at Corrie indicating several facets of his personality that she considered needed refining. Corrie told me that he had really intended for us to eat in town all the time.

We ate breakfast at Carson's Restaurant. We borrowed Alvin's truck. We found the whole pack of hounds along with Rough where we had cast them between Dean's Store and Kingsbury. We towed the truck into town for repairs.

I was happy to find Rough. In fact, it turned out that it was important that I found Rough. You see, a few months later I had to sell Ol' Rough to pay a debt. I got $75 for him. That $75 came within $5 of paying the hospital bill incurred when my oldest son was born. I guess it was not too bad a trade, a pretty good wolf dog for a new baby boy. At least I felt pretty good about it. After all, I had to only give $5 to boot on the deal.

The Hooch Ellis Bitches

Alvin Day, Perry Gary, and I were around a campfire drinking stale, warmed-over coffee and waiting for the hounds to come in. It was a fall morning in the early 1950s. The toll taken by cyanide guns set for coyotes, rattlesnakes, javelina, and old age had us short of coyote hounds. Our conversation was channeled toward a solution to our problem.

Alvin remembered that Hooch Ellis had a pair of inbred Dagwood pups, the accidental result of a sire-daughter mating. I did not know Hooch Ellis, but I did know Dagwood, a fine Walker hound that had won the South Texas Wolf Meet. Corrie Smith had bought him after he won at South Texas. He lost him when he tied him to the fence in front of his house after he came in from hunting one night. The sun came up the next morning, and by the time Corrie woke up Ol' Dagwood was dead of heatstroke. Good dog, careless hunter!

I met Hooch Ellis the next evening. His name was Houston Ellis. He was a giant of a man—tall, wide, and thick. I feel certain he would have weighed over three hundred pounds, and there was not a lot of fat involved. He lived on Tom Nance's ranch on the Blanco River about midway between Wimberly and San Marcos. He was a slow talker, and after a time he got around to saying he had a couple of Corrie Smith pups. We went and looked at them. They turned out to be as unlikely a looking pair of hounds as a wolf hunter ever saw. They were small, about midway in size between a beagle and a Walker hound. One was heavily built, the other slight. The heavy one had a tan head, black saddle back, a jug head, and a glass eye. The slim one was lemon and white with reddish lips and eyelids, heavy hair, and a flag tail. They both appeared to have been long on fleas and short on groceries for their whole lives.

Perry asked Mr. Ellis how much they had been hunted. Mr. Ellis replied that he got them as pups about two years before and that he had never had them in the woods. I was ready to offer him $15 for the pair with the hope that I could end up getting them for the $17 I had in my pocket. Perry was way ahead of me though. He offered to take the pups, start them and give them some experience, and only charge Mr. Ellis $5 apiece for doing it. In his slow way Mr. Ellis replied, "Why Perry, those pups are not worth $5." Perry replied that if that was the case we would take them off his hands and relieve him of the expense of feeding them. Mr. Ellis let us have the hounds.

They started easily after only a few nights of hunting. They showed to be just average pack dogs, not much speed and just average mouths. During the next year they were hunted three or four nights each week. They made every race, but they ran in back of the pack and their fine little chop mouths were drowned out by the other hounds. They were easy to handle, and seldom did we ever have to leave them in the woods. They were never individually named but referred to as the Hooch Ellis Bitches.

Perry came to me in the fall of 1953. He suggested that we make a week's hunt down on the Campbell ranch. Sounded good to me, so we started making plans. We got a group of our hunting friends to meet us down there on a Friday night. This gave us quite a gathering of hounds. The brag dogs in this bunch were Junior Herman's Bull, Jody Dupree's Molly, Hop Jackson's Buck and Honeybunch, Alvin Day's Dan and Happy, and my Rough. We had a total of over thirty hounds. Everyone went home Saturday morning except Perry and me. They left their hounds with us to hunt for the week. They were to come back to hunt the next Saturday night.

The weather was clear, cool, and beautiful. We divided the hounds into three packs. We tried to match them so that they would work the best. We ended up with a couple of brag dogs and about eight pack hounds in each pack. As best we could, we would run each pack for about eight hours and since coyotes were plentiful, the three packs gave us almost continuous running twenty-four hours a day. For the first couple of days the two packs that had been left in camp tied up would raise a racket in their desire to go to the running dogs.

Then along about Monday, I noticed the camp dogs were quiet and asleep on their stakeout chains while the others ran. By Tuesday all of the brag dogs were coming down lame from a diet of eight hours a day running; they also looked battered. The pack dogs were holding up to the running in better shape, probably because they were mostly smaller hounds, which caused their feet and legs to be less stressed than the larger brag dogs. Thursday we had a number of dogs that refused to run, so we divided the dogs that would run into two packs and did not run the daylight shift. Friday night we cast every hound we had in one pack. There was no foolishness left in any of these dogs. They ran as well as I ever heard a large pack run. After midnight the dogs started to quit and come in. By daylight there was not a brag dog left running, and all but about six of the pack dogs were back in camp. At good daylight we caught the handful of hounds still running. The Hooch Ellis Bitches were in this bunch. We did not tie up any dogs, just fed and watered them. Some would eat, though most refused food.

We were expecting our hunting friends to arrive just after dark Saturday evening. Our plans were to have a coyote race going when they arrived. Our problem was finding a hound that was not run out. We would put a lead rope on a hound and try to lead it out of camp to go hunting. Most would not stand up and walk even when dragged through cactus. Out of the whole bunch only two hounds would lead, the Hooch Ellis Bitches. Perry and I led one apiece out of camp and down toward a large earth tank. We had gone about three hundred yards when the bitch I was leading, the slim one, stuck her nose to the ground and switched her tail. I turned her aloose. She started working and opening on a hot coyote track. The bitch Perry was leading showed an interest, so Perry cut her aloose. She put in with her mate. In short order they had the track moving and in complete control. We went back to camp. In camp the only dog that showed any interest in the running dogs was a little red and white July hound of Perry's called TV. Perry walked TV toward the running Hooch Ellis Bitches, and in a short time ol' TV harked into the running bitches and went to work. We could not get another hound to run, not one.

Hop Jackson and Jody Dupree drove up into camp about the same time. Hop wanted to know why we did not have a race going.

We said we did if he would just listen. He asked why we did not turn Buck and Honeybunch to them. Perry told him that they were free to go if they wanted to. Hop walked around until he found his hounds. They were curled up in balls with their noses under their tails. He tried to stand Honeybunch up but she would not stand. Her eyes were blood red. Her feet had slipped all their pads. Her front end was a mass of slipped hair and cactus thorns. For the first time in her life all her ribs showed. Her gut was sucked up to her backbone. Hop was upset about her condition and even more upset when he found Buck in the same shape. He did not want to believe they had quit and were run out. He was abusive with Perry and me about the way we had treated them. He calmed down when we told him that the three running hounds had the same treatment but with almost twelve more hours of running.

By this time Alvin Day, Corrie Smith, and Emil Herman had arrived. Corrie wanted to know what dogs were running, since no one recognized their mouths. He seemed pleased when he found out that two of them were Dagwood pups.

Hop Jackson loaded up his hounds and left for home in a huff. Then Jody Dupree loaded his pack and headed home to Momma. Corrie and Emil decided they had business somewhere else, loaded, and left. That left Alvin, Perry, and me with eight or ten sleeping, run-out hounds, and three running ones. We drank coffee and listened to them until about 2 A.M. when we lay down on the ground and slept until daylight. At daylight Ol' TV was bedded down beside Perry. The two Hooch Ellis Bitches were still running. Alvin and I drove as close as we could to them, and I went out and caught them. They looked in pretty good shape and ate a big batch of dog food when we got them in camp. The bottoms of their feet were raw. There was not a lot hair left on their shoulders and legs. They had outrun some of the best hounds that money could buy.

One summer Perry hunted the Hooch Ellis Bitches along with TV and three other smaller type hounds he and Alvin had acquired. He hunted them four or five nights a week at the Roberts Ranch. They ran coyotes when they found one and jack rabbits the rest of the time. They got to where they could run down and catch a jack rabbit. Perry had them worked down hard as nails.

That fall Perry and Alvin carried them to the South Texas Wolf Meet. If memory serves, five of the six placed in the top ten hounds in the meet. Both the Hooch Ellis Bitches placed. Not bad when you consider they were not worth $5, were slow, had sorry mouths, and were inbred.

Neither of the bitches ever produced a pup that lived to maturity, and both of them disappeared out of races, probably victims of cyanide bombs, before they were six years old.

Over the years I have been asked many times about the gamest hound I ever heard run. My answer is always that I am not sure about the gamest hound I ever heard, but the two gamest hounds I have ever known were the Hooch Ellis Bitches. A splendid pair that were never appreciated enough to even be named.

What a waste that they were not bred to one of the better stud dogs of that time and a concentrated effort made to raise all their pups. However, in this day of limited hunting country, and running foxes in fenced in areas, it would be a waste to have a pack of hounds as game as the Hooch Ellis Bitches. Good game hounds today would be like some of us old hunters. They would not fit in this modern changing world.

Corrie Smith and Jack

Corrie Smith was a wolf hunter who did like to own a really good hound. I never sold him a hound, but it was my understanding that he would pay dearly for a hound that he thought was outstanding. Corrie, in the time I hunted with him, never raised a hound that ended up better than average. His way was to buy the already developed mature hound that had shown to be a good hound. He wanted the wolfhounds he bought to be fast, to have good mouths, and to be dead game. If Corrie could purchase a hound with all the above qualities that would also go in and fight a rundown coyote, then Ol' Corrie would really be high on him.

Now the second party in this tale was a most unlikely candidate to be the central character of a story. You see he was a hound. He was an ugly hound. And finally he was a hound that no one wanted. His name was Jack.

Jack was the most independent hound I ever knew. He had an ugly, coarse chop mouth. He was a Hudspeth foxhound. One of Eb Horner's good bitches whelped him. As a weaned pup, Eb gave him to Blackie Watkins. When he was about six months old, Blackie threw him in Alvin Day's dog pen. Blackie told Alvin that he was tired of feeding him. Alvin loaded him with his pack and took him hunting. He lost him that night and when he found him many weeks later the pup had learned how to run a varmint, had contracted canine distemper, and had lost about half of his body weight. In those pre-distemper vaccine days, a majority of the hounds that contracted distemper died. Jack was the only hound I ever knew that gained weight while he had distemper.

I always prided myself in my ability to break a hound from running off game, but I could not even get Jack's attention. Perry Lee Gary wore out several pairs of boots in his fruitless effort to break Jack. You could say that Ol' Jack was kind of bad to run a jack rabbit. He was so independent he would not quit a jackrabbit track to get in a pack of dogs running a wolf. Jack also had a habit of not homing in after a race; consequently, he was lost much of the time.

I remember one winter we hunted a couple of nights each week on the Campbell Ranch. Jack stayed aloose on that ranch from September to the following March doing for the most part what he did best, running jack rabbits. Occasionally he would fall in with our pack and run a coyote. Other times we would hear him running by himself. We would see him from time to time, thin as a rail but otherwise healthy. He simply could make his own living off the land. When he ran with our pack, if the race lasted more than a couple of hours, you could bet he would be at the front of the pack with Dan, Molly, and Rough. He was fearless, and anytime a coyote turned on the pack, Ol' Jack would lock up with him.

Corrie Smith bought a whole pack of six hounds from Arlie Hughes in South Texas. Corrie paid dearly for the pack, and his enthusiasm for them spilled over to Alvin, Perry, and me in the form of bragging about the wonderful ability of the pack. Corrie was pretty optimistic about how his new pack would measure up to our hounds. Corrie laid up his new pack for a few days after he got them and fed them all the high-priced dog food they wanted. When they were slick enough to suit him, he insisted that we make a hunt with them to the Campbell Ranch.

We made camp in the middle of a county dirt road on a tall chalk hill when we got there. Camp consisted of a mesquite fire and a pot of coffee. As we drank coffee, Corrie told us that if any of us had a single hound that barked between his pack and the wolf that night, he would buy breakfast for all of us. If I turned my head just right and strained my ears, I could hear Ol' Jack way off to the northwest running a jack rabbit and pouring out that ugly chop mouth of his. We had lost him there on the Campbell Ranch on our last hunt several weeks before.

In due course a coyote howled close to camp. We cast my Rough, Jody Dupree's White Man, and Hop Jackson's Buck. They went to the barking wolf and put him to running. We fed hounds into the pack one or two at a time until we had all our hounds in the race. I remember it as being a large pack of probably more than twenty hounds. They put so much pressure on the coyote that he decided to leave that part of the world, heading northwest. We tried to follow in trucks but there were just no roads to get us within hearing of the hounds. We came back to camp, drank coffee, and told hunting stories. Occasionally someone would drive off to see if they could hear the pack. At two or three in the morning, I decided that sleep would fit my needs better than twice warmed over coffee and tales. So I pitched my G. I. blanket down on the ground and went to sleep.

Sometime later, at daybreak, I awoke with a start. I could hear the pack coming into hearing from the east. I looked around and saw that everyone was asleep. I hollered at them as I poked up the fire and put on the coffee pot.

The pack kept coming toward us, and as they got closer they made a steady roar as each hound gave mouth on the track. From the top of the chalk hill I could see a long way. After a bit I spotted the coyote as he scurried through the brush ahead of the pack. He was fifty or sixty yards ahead of the first hound, Ol' Jack, closely followed by Rough, Molly, and Dan. Then came the rest of the hounds all strung out with Corrie's new pack mixed in with the last hounds.

The coyote was headed in a direction to cross the county road just down from our camp. I hurried to the point I thought the coyote would come out. Before I had gone halfway, the coyote came out on the road. I could tell this was a rundown coyote about to be caught. He saw me as he entered the road, which caused him to turn down the road away from me for a way before he cut back into the brush on the same side he had come from. About that time Jack came out on the road. He turned with the coyote scent and headed down the road. He had only gone a few yards when he came to an old traffic-killed jack-rabbit hull that had been pounded by traffic and sun and air dried until it was only a flat slab of rawhide. Jack scooped up the hide as he went by and started wolfing it down as he continued after the coyote. I caught him just as he swallowed the hide.

I started dragging him back to camp and, at the same time, hollering at Corrie to make sure he recognized that hounds were between the coyote and his new pack. Corrie was jumping up and down and red in the face because my dragging Ol' Jack back into the pack had messed up the coyote scent and caused the dogs to lose the track. He screamed at me to turn Jack aloose so we could catch the coyote. I took Jack on into camp and made Corrie agree that Jack was ahead of his new pack and that he owed us breakfast. The hounds never recovered the line. We did not catch the coyote, and a short time after that we loaded up and started home

Alvin stopped at the only cafe in Campbellton. I told Perry to order two ham and egg breakfasts for me. I did not come in until the owner set the food on the table. Then I dragged in Ol' Jack. I sat him right up in a chair and put an order of ham and eggs in front of him. Jack wolfed them down. Corrie realized what was happening. As Corrie started to object, I told him that since Jack earned the breakfast, he (Corrie) had no choice other than to pay for it. Corrie got a little red in the face and remarked that Jack smelled so bad that he was ruining his breakfast. None of the other hunters, Alvin, Hop, Jody, Perry, or I would agree with him. About that time the owner of the cafe stated that if we ever expected to come back in that place again we would have to get that stinking dog out of there right then. I took Jack out and loaded him in the dog box. Corrie, good sport that he was, paid up even for Jack, and we went home.

Some weeks after this hunt Perry told me that he had traded Jack off to a Louisiana hunter for a young hound. We were all glad to see him gone because his rabbit running was spoiling our young hounds.

A couple of years later Perry and I were hunting at Gander Slew out of Luling. It was a beautiful night, cold, still, and clear. Before our hounds started a coyote, a hound came running into hearing. Its big, ugly, coarse chop mouth could only belong to Jack. Our pack started a coyote and ran it right over the single dog. When our pack had gone far enough to hear again we could tell that Jack had come through them and was still running his rabbit.

I asked Perry how he thought Jack had gotten back to central Texas from Louisiana. Perry's answer was that just maybe he had run a jack rabbit the whole three hundred miles. None of us ever heard or heard of Jack again, but to this day I will bet that no one ever broke Jack off of rabbits or that Jack ever did anything other than his own way.

As I said, Jack was the most independent hound I have ever known, and deep down in my heart I kind of respected and admired him.

It Don't Take as Much Water

My little 1948 red Ford pickup truck was sick. Weird noises came up from under the hood. A greasy cloud of foul glop poured forth from the exhaust pipe. The transmission would jump out of gear at the rate of four jumps to the mile. The tires were slick. I was just about afoot.

Perry Lee Gary came by the house at dark one evening late in the winter of 1954. I thought he had come by to suggest that we go run a coyote that night. Instead, he told me that he had just bought me a fresh wrecked Ford car, 1947 variety. He explained that he had bought the whole thing for $15. Perry knew me well. He knew I could not do things mechanical. He also knew I was in my usual state of teetering on the edge of financial calamity. Before I had a chance to protest, he explained that the wrecked car had an excellent motor and transmission in it and that we were going to install them in my truck. Sure we were!

We went that night and loaded my truck with everything we could get off the wrecked car: lights, wheels, radiator, tires, engine, transmission, and other parts I could not identify.

Perry got an "A" frame and a chain hoist, and Sunday morning at daylight he attacked my truck. In a few hours he had the front off and the sick vital organs removed from my poor little truck. As he started back in with fresh parts from the wrecked car, he found that nothing wanted to fit. He had to remove the internal workings from the car transmission and thread them on the old drive shaft in the truck housing. This was necessitated by the fact that the power shaft from the transmission of the car would not fit on the drive shaft of the truck. I got a sick feeling when he completed the exchange because there was about a pint of transmission parts left over. The clutch housing for the truck's transmission did not want to fit onto the car engine. I do not know how he solved this problem because every time I got close to the disaster he would snarl at me to get out of his way.

Perry worked in a frenzy till midnight that Sunday. Then each night after that he would show up at the house after work and continue his efforts. As I started to work the next Saturday, Perry showed up to work on the truck. When I came in that night my truck was in the driveway. It looked good because it was all back together. Perry, Ellie, and their girls were in the house. Perry was drinking coffee and telling funny stories to Billye, Ellie, and our combined children.

Perry took me for a drive. The new engine in my truck purred like a kitten. The transmission did what transmissions do. We loaded all the unused remains on my truck. Monday I took the mess to Dutch Meyer's Junk Yard. There I was able to make a trade wherein Dutch got my junk and in return I got two perfectly good used tires. These two tires coupled with two from the wreck, gave me a fine set on the truck.

My natural inclination was to baby my truck after that. I had no confidence that it would hold together. Perry, on the other hand, encouraged me to use it hard. He contended that it was in fine shape. I was sure in no position to argue the point with him.

Several months passed. Then one day in the spring of 1955 Perry came by and informed me we were going on a fox hunt in East Texas. He said Paulie Mutschler from Westhoff, Texas, was going with us. Sounded good to me, so I asked how we were going to get there. Perry replied that the only reason he had asked me to go was to use my truck and have me as camp cook. He said he had just been on a hunt for five days, and they had eaten bacon and eggs every meal. He informed me that I was not to serve bacon and eggs on this hunt.

I took a week off from work. We borrowed every hound we could from our hunting friends. We ended up with a total of thirteen hounds. Some of them came from Alvin Day, Corrie Smith, Jody Dupree, Ben Marks, and Hop Jackson. We loaded bedding and cooking gear into my truck, hooked on a dog trailer, and loaded the hounds in it. We went to Paulie's house at Westhoff.

The next morning Paulie threw his gear in my truck along with a good-sized wall tent. Paulie had four hounds. We loaded all seventeen hounds in the trailer and left for somewhere in East Texas. Perry said he would drive. The speed limit at that time, as I remember, was sixty miles per hour. My loaded truck pulling a trailer of hounds would go about eighty miles an hour. That is just how fast Perry drove. He said he wanted to show me how good a job he had done on the truck. It held together just fine. We drove into Diball, Texas, in the middle of the afternoon.

There was a factory building at Diball that was about fifty yards off the highway. It made broom handles. Perry saw a man beside the building. He pulled up and asked the man where we could go to hunt in that area. It just so happened the man was a fox hunter. He told us to take a dirt road to the east, go to the end of it and to camp, and hunt where it pleased us. The country sure looked good. Central Texas was suffering from a drought, but this country was green and wet.

We went to the end of the road. We drove into the heavily timbered forest until we were stopped by a creek. The creek made a U bend, which gave us the creek on three sides. There was a beautiful variety of trees in this bend of the creek: oaks and hickory sprinkled in among groves of pines. Paulie chose a spot in the grove of pine trees to set up his tent. I picked a spot across a clearing from the tent under a huge oak to build my cook fire. There was plenty of solid, dead oak wood within fifty yards of camp for my fire. Perry found some boards that were the remains of an old pen used, we were told, to hold mules at a time when the timber was worked with mules. Perry took my ax and in short order had constructed a rough dining table and bench from the boards. I found an old sheet of tin roofing. I took it to the creek and put it half in and half out of the creek. We would walk into the water on the tin and bathe with a bar of P & G laundry soap. The flow gave us fresh water to rinse. We could then walk out on the dry tin to dress and not be bothered with muddy feet. We wallowed in the luxury of the tent, the table, the bench, and the bath. The hounds were put out on two stakeout chains.

By the time the sun went down, camp was made, the dogs had been watered, and I had a supper of beef stew and Dutch-oven cornbread ready. I had bought a fifty-pound block of ice in Diball. We did not have an icebox, so I put the ice in a cardboard box, then that box in a bigger box, and that box in a still larger box. I dug a hole and buried the whole thing under a tree. Each evening I would dig up the ice and chip off enough for iced tea. We had never had iced tea in camp before, and we really enjoyed it. The ice lasted about three days.

At dark each night we would cast the hounds. They were usually able to start a fox close to camp. In all honesty, we put down a pretty sorry lot of hounds. Paulie's coyote pack had never run a fox before and Perry and I had gathered up mostly castoffs and culls. Foxes were plentiful, so when the dogs lost a fox they were able to start another one easily. We would stay up all night listening to the hounds and then sleep during the day. I would serve a big breakfast after good daylight. The hounds would start drifting into camp about daylight, and usually by 10 A.M. they had all homed in and were fed, watered, and staked out for the day. We would then go to sleep and sleep most of the day. I would get up in the middle of the afternoon and start cooking our supper. I had a good set of cast-iron pots, a skillet, a large covered pot, and a Dutch oven. I also had a large granite coffee pot that rounded out my cooking gear. This cooking gear left me with no limitation on what I could prepare. I served some form of hot bread fresh out of the Dutch oven almost every meal. I think we ate well, and as per Perry's instructions I did not serve a single fried egg or piece of bacon.

An event happened in this camp that was one of the strangest that ever happened to me in any camp. I started telling this tale thirty years ago, and over the years I have had it come back to me a number of times. Details have been changed to fit the circumstances of the narration but the basic punch line remains intact. I can only state that the following events happened to me on a spring day in 1955. They happened in a small clearing in the bend of a creek at the end of a dirt road due east of Diball, Texas.

I had gotten up to start my preparation of the evening meal. Perry and Paulie were asleep in the tent. I had finished making a pot of coffee and was drinking a cup of the fresh brew. It was good. As I sat on a log and drank my coffee, I got the feeling that I was being watched. I looked over my shoulder to the south and saw a man on a black horse watching me from the edge of the clearing. I judged the man's age to about sixty years or so. He wore tattered and patched overalls and a long-sleeved chambray shirt. He wore tiny gold-rimmed spectacles and a straw hat. He was a small man and I would guess his height to be about five feet, six inches. My guess was that he would weigh less than 140 pounds. The saddle on his horse was the absolute worst saddle I have ever seen in use. It was of a style used in the late 1800s or early 1900s, small high pommel, narrow fork with no swell, an extremely high straight cantle, and large square skirts. Each piece of leather in the saddle appeared to have fallen off and had been reattached with baling wire, binder twine, cotton string, shingle nails, or any other material handy.

It was difficult to look at the man or the saddle because under the saddle was one of the finest saddle mares I have ever seen. My first thought was that she was at least half Arabian, and I still think that to be the case. I judged her to be some 14 or 14½ hands tall, and I could not find a flaw in her conformation. She was coal black and her coat shone enough that I got the feeling a man could shave by looking at his reflected image from her skin. She was not shod but her hooves were well trimmed. Her mane and tail showed daily attention.

The man broke the silence by asking if I had seen any cattle. I replied that we had been there several days and that we had seen none. He replied that he was missing several head. I repeated that we had neither seen any cattle nor seen any sign of cattle.

The man got down from his horse and dropped the rope reins. He walked up to the fire, picked up Perry's cup, and poured himself a cup of my freshly brewed coffee. He took one sip and poured the cup of coffee on the ground. He picked up my pot of fresh coffee and emptied it on the ground. He then filled the pot about ¼ full with fresh water and added the biggest part of a whole can of coffee. He stirred up the fire and sat the pot on the coals. I was so surprised by his actions that I just stood there and gaped at him.

In a bit the pot came to a boil. He poured out a cup and quickly drank it. He cleared his throat and said, "You know, it don't take near as much water to make coffee as some folks think it does."

He turned, walked to his horse, mounted, and rode through camp and into the brush. I could only stand and stare after him.

Finally I woke Perry and Paulie. I related to them what had happened. I showed them the pile of grounds where the man poured out the pot of coffee. I showed them the horse tracks through camp. I doubt I ever convinced them that the man had actually acted as he did.

A couple of days later we broke camp and went home. Even though we had not put down a good pack of foxhounds, we each agreed that this was one of the most pleasant hunts we had ever made. We had camped in beautiful country. The weather had been nearly perfect. Insects and the usual assortment of pests had never been a serious problem. There had been an abundance of foxes to run. We had not lost any hounds. There had been plenty of good food. We had enjoyed each other's company. We had had enough time to really get a feel of the country.

Actually had it not been for the little man, the black mare, and the pot of coffee, I doubt that I would have even remembered the hunt. Hunting trips are best remembered for the catastrophes and disasters, not for having an easy time.

Now you take the time Perry and I lost his car along with all our food in a flooded creek while hunting on the Campbell Ranch. The third day after we lost our food, we ended up eating a bobcat Old Lady and Streak had treed. Son, I can really remember that hunt.

I Thought She Was Your Wife

The first time I saw her she was in a crowd of people, but even then I could tell that she was a lady with class. She normally would not have caught my eye being a bit small and a trifle frail for my taste. I think it was probably the look she gave me as I passed, an aloof, regal look, that lingered with me long after I should have forgotten her. I worked my way back through the crowd in an effort to get another glimpse of her. Suddenly there she was, the center of attention of a group of men, her raven black hair glistening in the sunlight. My mind raced off in a wild fantasy as I looked at her, a dream that had me joyfully frolicking with her over the countryside. I am getting a little ahead of myself here, but even in my fantasy I would not allow myself to consider that this dream could become a reality. It did though and as a matter of fact I spent more nights with her for the next two years than I did my wife.

Royce Parrish, a total stranger, walked up beside me shattering the bubble of my dreams. He told me the little registered Black and Tan bitch could be mine for $75. He might as well have said $10,000. I was attending the second Texas State Championship Wild Coon Hunt at Mexia, Texas. I had only the money left in my pocket to pay for enough 23¢-per-gallon gasoline to get me the 170 miles home. Yep, my $2 would get me back home, but the trick was to convince my stomach that it did not need food for the next three days. How was I to know that they would charge a fortune, ten or twelve dollars as I remember, to enter a hound in a wild coon hunt? Oh well, I had my coffee pot and a part of a pound of coffee. Minor details, as I remember, were not made for young men to worry over.

Night by night the hunt progressed. I was pleased with the showing Shotsie made as she was never more than a handful of points away from the leaders. Saturday morning, after the first night's hunt, I got up and put on a pot of coffee. Mr. Parrish walked up and again tried to sell me the Black and Tan bitch. I explained my financial situation to him. I not only did not have extra money with me, I did not have any reserves anywhere else. I got the feeling Mr. Parrish got my message because he did not mention the sale of the bitch to me again. That is, not until Sunday afternoon late, when he again walked into my camp. He had a box in his hands and he asked if I had any coffee. I poured. He opened. That box contained the most beautiful coconut cake that I have ever seen. My minor detail of hunger came into sharp focus at that moment.

Sometime later, at the end of the cake and coffee, he asked if I would take the bitch and send him the money when I could. I asked what would happen if the bitch did not suit me. He answered to do with her as I saw fit and send nothing in payment to him. I replied that under those conditions I would take the bitch but only if he would lower his price to $50. He looked at the ground for a long time, choked back his first answer, and agreed to my terms. We shook hands and the deal was finished. I then asked why, if the bitch was of any value, he had worked so hard to get rid of her. His wife, he told me, was in the laying hen business. This black bitch killed every chicken that came within her reach. His instructions when he left home were to get rid of the bitch or not bother to return home. Since his wife had baked the cake I had just eaten, I could better understand his dilemma. She was a cook.

The hunt ended Sunday night, and as I remember, Shotsie finished well up in the top ten in the grade class. She was not my hound, but I had asked her owner, Gus Eoff, to let me run her because she was the best in our area. I was interested in seeing what an organized wild coon hunt was like, and I wanted to see how our best hound compared to hounds from all over the country.

After I got back home, I kept the news of my new hound to myself because I did not want any of my hunting friends laughing at me because of my having a hound that a stranger had sold to me on credit. I looked her over carefully. She was four years old and could only have weighed forty-two pounds soaking wet. She had good feet, good straight legs, a good back, a deep chest, a good head, and nice medium ears. Instead of the usual pumpkin seeds of tan over the eyes of a Black and Tan, this bitch had a whole mask of tan that extended down over the muzzle. She was quiet in the pen and would eat anything put before her. So far, so good.

The first night home I went to the woods with her. She did pretty well. She had a beautiful clear chop and squall on the trail. She gave plenty of mouth, but she was clean in its use, opening only when making forward progress. At the tree her mouth changed to a killing chop, and she treed with her front feet on the tree. The first coon she showed me was a small one, and she had it dead before I could get out of the tree. She had not done quite as well as I thought Shotsie would have done, but I felt good about her performance. The second night she did much better. She hunted harder and wider. She ran with confidence. When a coon went up, she located quickly and her treeing left me with the impression that she was going to cut the tree down.

The third night I put her on some spoiled coons close to the community of Golly. It was a country of turned out fields with lots of trees along old fence lines. Those coons would run well, and when they went up they would travel through the trees on a fence line until they could come down and leave without the hound knowing they were gone. The first coon she treed pulled this trick, but as I walked to the tree I could hear her move, still treeing, with the coon as he traveled through the trees. As best I could make out, she went with him forty yards or so and she held him to the tree. This was the first time I ever saw a hound do this. She put on a show for me that night, showing me six coons in an area where in the past good hounds had to be lucky to show me one, I knew I had a good one. One good enough that even Shotsie would be hard pressed to stay with.

I hunted my new bitch Monday, Tuesday, and Wednesday nights. Each night she showed great improvement. Thursday morning I went to the bank. I asked Bob Pollard for a fifty-dollar loan. He asked if I had a co-signer for the note, and I replied, "No." He asked if I had collateral for the loan. Again I had to reply, "No." He asked how he could know that I would repay the loan. My answer was because I gave him my word on it. He asked what the loan was for. I told him to buy a hound. He paused for a bit, looked me in the eye, sighed, and filled out some papers. I had my first bank loan. As quickly as the

U. S. Post Office got it to him, Mr. Parrish had $50, and I owned my first registered coonhound.

Central Texas in the mid-'50s was under the influence of a terrible drought. For five years, each succeeding year had delivered less rain. Seed for planted crops did not germinate from lack of moisture. Range land failed to support grass. Rivers stopped flowing. Trees died. During the winters of 1955 and 1956 I hunted all night, many nights without ever seeing a blade of grass. Dust would boil up around my ankles as I walked, and each cold front would bring with it clouds of choking, thick, yellow, West Texas dust. Coon hunters with good hounds would hunt for nights without their hounds being able to tree a coon. It was simply too dry for their hounds to smell coon scent. I went into the worst of these years with my new Black and Tan bitch. Each night I hunted her, I felt she got better. The better she got, the harder I hunted her. As a matter of fact, as I started to go hunting one night, my wife stopped me. She told me that since I had hunted for thirty straight nights, I was going to take her out that night. I did!

I judge a coonhound on how well it hunts and finds coons, on how well it can trail the coon, on how well it can locate the tree the coon went up, and how it performs on a tree. There are coonhounds that hunt hard but never seem to start their share of coons. There are hounds that do not hunt. There are hounds that hunt so hard that many times they are out of hearing when they start. None of these hounds suit me. I want a hound to hunt diligently, but with me. I want it to go to the coon and not waste time looking where coons are not likely to be. My new bitch did just that. There are hounds that cannot run a track well enough to be able to tree many, if any, coons. Some hounds potter on the track to the point that they just cannot push the coon up a tree. There are a few hounds that are so fast and accurate in their trail work that races only last a few minutes. None of these types suits me. I expect a coonhound to be accurate in its trail work and just fast enough to encourage the coon to run before it goes up. I have always hunted for the sport of it. To me a good part of the sport is the race. My new bitch would tree the coon, but she always seemed to be able to get a race out of him before he went up. Some hounds, after a coon goes up, have a hard time locating the tree he went up. Some locate quickly but do not check to see if the coon has come down. As a result these hounds will show you many bare trees. A really good locator will bark up quickly, carefully check to see if the coon has come down, and only then settle down on the tree. My new bitch did just that. To me a really good tree hound has a big change in mouth from trail to tree. To me a really good tree hound should give a lot of mouth at the tree. A good tree dog is not jealous of the tree and will not fight other hounds at the tree. And finally, a good tree dog will stay treed until I get to the tree. My new hound was a really good tree dog.

In the fifty-five years that I have run hounds, I have hunted with and against hundreds of foxhounds and thousands of coonhounds. I have judged thousands of beagles in licensed field trials run in brace, small pack, and large pack. This Black and Tan bitch had the best nose I have ever seen on a hound. To go with this nose, she had the patience, determination, and gameness to use it to its best advantage. The best of noses is wasted if the hound lacks these characteristics.

As I stated before, I owned her at the height of a terrible drought. I hunted her with every hound or pack of hounds I could get her down with. Night after night she would tree coons that good hounds could not open on. On the good nights, when the hounds could run, she usually ran to the back of the pack, but I began to notice that the fast hounds could not beat her to the tree. I remember an instance when a man's hound beat her to a tree once. The man bragged about it for almost a year. Gus Eoff and I were hunting one night when we had a split. His pack went one way, my black bitch the other. We went with his pack. I lost my bitch that night, but late the next afternoon Poncho Esquivel came in from the Scrutchin Ranch and told me that she was treed in a draw down from his house. He said she treed just before he started to bed at 10 P.M. I got to her after sundown the following day. She had been on the tree for more than twenty hours. It was August. The thermometer had gone over 100 that day. When I drove up to Poncho's house she was still pouring out that killing chop mouth like a clock ticking. Son, that is a tree dog.

In the two years I owned this bitch she treed more than a thousand coons each year for me. No man can say he ever went to the woods with her that she failed to tree coons.

I can remember only one bare tree she showed me in those two years. That is remarkable when one considers that the average coonhound will show you that many in a single night. I can remember a number of times when she would make me return again and again to a tree until I would finally find the coon somewhere in the tree. I shook coons out on her until her whole head was a mass of scar tissue from fighting them. Fresh bites on this tissue would bleed badly and this flow of blood was hard to stop.

My little bitch had the ability to pull a sorry pack of dogs together and make them look good. Hounds that could not trail well enough to run a coon to a tree looked great when they were down with her. I saw dogs that would not normally hold a tree try to eat a tree up when they were with my bitch. Really good hounds never looked their best with her. She corrected every mistake they made on the track or on the tree. The constant pressure of this correction made good hounds erratic in their work and more prone to mistakes, which led to more corrections, which led to more mistakes. I was amused when owners of good hounds would pick up their hounds and go home to momma because of the way my bitch made their hounds look. Those owners were not prone to say many good things about my bitch.

I only have one picture of this bitch. I looked at this picture as I got into writing this. As I thought back on old hounds and old hunts and old friends, I was caught up in a tide of nostalgia. It was sweet to remember how my bitch made chills run up my back when she ran a coon, and how, when she treed, she would make the hair stand up on the back of my neck.

My experience is that if one wants to raise good hounds one must breed good bitches to the best dogs available. If one raises between thirty and forty of these pups, he will most likely come up with a fairly good prospect. If one wants an outstanding hound, he must be prepared to go through at least a thousand pups from good sires and dams. These figures sound a little high to you? Check around. I think they will hold true for hounds, bird dogs, racehorses, and maybe even humans.

My wonderful little bitch died in January of 1957. She died because of my stupidity and ignorance. I had bred her to an average Black and Tan hound. I bred to an average hound because I could not afford the stud fee to a good one. In light of what I know now, I know that she was eaten up with hookworms and whipworms. I ran her all night five or six nights every week. Two nights before she whelped I shook a tremendous coon out on her. This coon worked her head over before she and I killed him. Because of the scar tissue involved I could not stop the flow of blood from cuts received in this fight. She lost a great deal of blood. She had four pups, but again in my ignorance I did not realize that she had retained the fifth pup inside of her. The combination of overwork, weakness from parasites, loss of blood from wounds, and infection from the retained pup were too much for her. She died four days after she whelped.

The final judgment on the greatness of a hound is if it can reproduce quality hounds. One bitch pup survived from her only litter. This pup made the second best hound I ever followed. In turn this pup was bred once and only one bitch pup survived from her litter. This pup was bred and produced McDonald's Big John. Big John won the World's Championship for the breed in 1964. So a pedigree would show that Taylor's Black Ruby produced Taylor's Black Ruby II, who produced Taylor's Maid, who produced McDonald's Big John. The bitches behind Big John, for one reason or another, were sole survivors. I did not have thirty or forty pups to choose from, only what was left. I think their ability to reproduce speaks for itself.

I did not breed Ruby. I did not train her. All I did was to hunt her enough for her full potential to develop. I do not know if she could have beaten the great night hunt hounds of that era because she never had the opportunity to compete with them. But you know, time has shown that the truly great hounds of her day could not reproduce quality hounds. While I had her, I hunted her against every good hound I could afford to get her to. I never saw her equal. You may take this with a grain of salt, because hounds like people, do seem to get better after they are dead. But after her death, I did hunt with and against the great hounds. I honestly never saw her equal.

In my two-year association with Ruby, she gave me a lot. She gave me what I feel was equivalent to a college education in hound work. She gave me the opportunity to meet people like

Clarence Echols, C. C. Hancock, and H. A. Wallace, who I found to be that rare blend of houndman, sportsman, and gentleman. A study of today's Black and Tan hounds shows she made a major contribution to the breed. She gave me more hunting pleasure than one man deserves. She gave me the second best hound I ever followed. And finally, she never gave me less than her best. Not bad, considering she was too small, killed chickens, and was only a $50 hound.

Allen Smith was a friend. The worst that could be said about Allen was that he was a gentle, kind, intelligent man. To my knowledge he never went to the woods with a hound. I first met him during the time I hunted Ruby, and we usually had coffee together at least once a week. Several years ago Allen was in bed at his home in Pearsall, Texas, in the process of dying of bone cancer. He had reached the point where life revolved around the time lapse between shots for pain. I stayed with him for a time in a futile effort to ease his discomfort. During this time our conversations covered myriad topics. In the early hours of one morning he told me that he had something that he had meant to tell me for a long time. He then related that he had come to know how much I had thought of Ruby and that he had thought more of me because of the respect and admiration I had shown for her in our conversations. He said that he had felt great sadness and remorse when I told him I had lost her. He said that even though he had known me for over a year, it was not until weeks later in a conversation with a mutual friend, that he had learned that Ruby was a hound. "Taylor," he said, "I always thought she was your wife."

Allen, old friend, she may not have been my wife, but believe me she was a lady with almost as much class.

Mose White and Rachel

Mose White was a coon hunter. I never did know him very well, but I have a hazy recollection that he was a bricklayer. When I first met him, I think he lived in Austin. I met him at some organized wild coon hunt. I remember hunting against him, and I remember that he ran a fine English coonhound bitch named Rachel. Rachel was the kind of hound every coon hunter dreams of owning.

One afternoon in the winter of probably 1957, I took a break from work at the feed store and went for coffee at Carson's Restaurant on Interstate 35 at San Marcos. When I walked into the restaurant I spotted Mose White drinking a cup of coffee. It had been a year or so since we had seen each other, so we spent an enjoyable fifteen or twenty minutes catching up with each other's activities. Seems Ol' Mose had just finished some job he had been working on, and he was on his way home. I asked about Rachel, and he told me that she was about the same as ever. Mose was not one to brag on his hound. Said he planned to get in more hunting as he had moved from Austin to a place on the Colorado River out of Bastrop. He invited Ruby and me to come hunt with him on the coming Saturday night.

I jumped at the chance because I sure welcomed the opportunity to run Ruby with a quality hound like Rachel. I wanted to see how my young hound compared with the more experienced Rachel. After I lost Ol' Ruby, I had watched her only surviving pup, Taylor's Black Ruby II, through the process of starting to run and starting to tree. The young Ruby was a completely different hound from her mother. She was strong on the track and a little weak on the tree. I thought she showed great promise, but I really needed to test her with one of the better hounds. I considered Rachel to be the best hound in Central Texas at that time.

Before dark that Saturday night I loaded Ruby and left with a sketchy set of directions to Mose's new home on the Colorado River. I may not be too good at finding a doctor's office in a strange city. I usually have great difficulty in finding a convention center in some distant city. It is always a struggle for me to find some special ladies store in almost any town. But, you tell me about some obscure fishing hole on some creek no one ever heard of, and I can go directly to it. Tell me about a rifle I really would like to own in some rundown pawnshop somewhere in Amarillo, Texas, and without a conscious thought I will end up parked in front of that pawnshop with hardly a crook in my trail getting there. Mose told me he lived six or seven miles northwest of Bastrop on the Colorado River. I drove straight to his house.

We cast Ruby and Rachel at Mose's backyard gate which was only a stone's throw from the Colorado River. It was one of those special nights where at sundown you could tell it was going to frost or freeze that night. It was one of those special hunting nights where there was not a perceptible hint of a breeze. It was one of those perfect nights where the only sounds heard were the sounds of the river, the sounds of the hunter's feet in the winter leaves, and the sounds of the hounds as they went about their business. I knew Rachel's mouth. Mose quickly learned Ruby's mouth. You would think we would have let the dogs talk for themselves, but we did not. No, we could not! When Ruby struck first, I had to tell Mose, "Ruby is struck." After a bit Mose said, and I feel he just had to, "I believe Rachel is a little out front." And after a short time, it just poured out of me, "I think Ruby has taken over the lead." Then Mose said, "Sounds like that ol' coon is taking them across the river." And shortly thereafter I cried, "Listen to Ruby hit that tree!" And Mose replied, "Yeh, Rachel is on it hard too."

We walked down the river several hundred yards to where the dogs were treed across the river. I shone my big light across the river into the branches of the big sycamore tree the dogs were treeing. The coon showed me his eyes instantly. I asked Mose where a bridge was to cross the river. He said the closest bridge was six or seven miles at Bastrop, which would mean a six or seven mile walk from Bastrop back to the tree. I asked Mose if he had a boat. He replied, "No." I asked how we were going to get our dogs back across the river. Mose shouted, "Come here, Rachel." That damn bitch left the tree, hit the water, and swam straight across to Mose. He put his lead on her. I called Ruby, I screamed at Ruby, I cursed Ruby, I begged Ruby, I pleaded with Ruby. That black slut stood with her front feet on that tree barking up like a clock ticking.

I walked down and felt the water. It was ice cold. I asked Mose if he would cast Rachel. I was hoping that when she struck and started running that maybe Ruby would leave the tree and hark into her. He did and she did, and when Rachel shortly treed the second coon Ruby stayed on her tree, treeing like her life depended on it. I told Mose I would have to swim the river to get Ruby. He took Rachel off her tree, and we walked back to where Ruby was treeing. I took off my coat, my shirt, my T-shirt, my shoes, my socks, my pants, and my shorts. That left me standing there in the cold winter air stark naked except for a rope lead around my neck.

I do not know for certain how wide the Colorado River is six or seven miles northwest of Bastrop, but since you will, most likely, not know either, I will state that it is more than fifty yards wide. Well me and that dog lead hit that cold winter water and across we went. I put the lead on Ruby, and the dog, the lead, and I started back across the river. That river water felt even colder without the lead rope around my neck to keep me warm. And do you think that blamed bitch would help me swim? All she would do was to try to jerk me back to that tree she had been on. Finally I won the struggle and dragged her up the bank to my clothes, but she won the round: She had saved all the water in her hair to shake off on my pile of clothes. I pulled on my wet clothes over my totally wet body. When I finished, I was shivering from cold as hard as I ever did when I had malaria on Makin Island in the Pacific.

I told Mose I needed to do some hard walking to warm myself. We cast the hounds. I set a torrid pace down the river. That's when we found the fish trap piled up in amongst a bunch of driftwood high up on the riverbank. Mose stated he wanted the trap, and proceeded to tear into the drift to get it. I tried to persuade Mose into leaving the fish trap. I reasoned that it would only get him in trouble with the game warden. Mose said, "What fish trap? Man don't you know an armadillo trap when you see one?" I then asked how he would explain his armadillo trap set out in the Colorado River. Mose told me I was the dumbest hunter he had ever been to the woods with. He said, "Don't you know that when an armadillo goes to cross a river he just lets out his breath, sinks to the bottom, and walks across the river? Hell man! What better place to set the trap than out in the river?" I just stood there, waiting and shivering.

The dogs struck. By this time Mose had the trap out on top of the drift. We left it there and followed the dogs. The coon and the hounds proceeded to put on one of the finest races I have ever listened to. The coon went back and forth across the river. He tapped trees and left. He went out in the brush on both sides of the river. I knew that ol' coon had been run before. He knew every trick. Those two bitches just inhaled his tracks and put tremendous pressure on him. By the time the coon gave up and went up a tree on the far side of the river, I could tell that Ruby was "having a little of the best of it" with Rachel. Man! That almost made me forget I was freezing cold.

When we got even with the hounds who were both treeing hard on the far side of the river, Mose said, "Come here Rachel." Ol' Rachel came straight across to Mose. He put his lead on her. I did not waste any breath calling Ruby. I shucked my clothes. I hung her lead around my neck. I swam to the far bank, put the lead on Ruby, and fought her all the way back across the river. She remembered not to shake the water out of her hair until we got to my pile of clothes. I was shaking so hard I could not button my shirt. My teeth chattered so hard I could not hear what Mose said. He cast Rachel, so I cast Ruby.

Ruby struck out about a quarter-mile down the river. That coon would make a long run and cross the river. Then another long run and cross the river. Even though I was as cold as I was I could tell that my young Ruby was getting some bit more than half the work done as compared to the more experienced Rachel. Hot damn! I almost forgot how cold I was again. The bitches hit the tree—on the far side of the river. Mose called, "Come in Rachel." She came straight in. I slowly undressed, hung the lead around my neck, and swam the river. I caught Ruby and started fighting her across the river.

I was almost paralyzed from cold. My mind started to slow down. My arms and legs would hardly work. I wanted to quit. Quit? I kept telling myself, you do not tolerate *quit* in your hounds—how can you quit? I made myself struggle on. At that time I had never heard of hypothermia. Believe me, I had a big dose of it. I finally got to the bank. Mose took Ruby. My feet and legs were so cold I could not tell when they were touching the ground. I stumbled and fell, got up, and stumbled and fell. I got to my clothes. My hands would hardly work enough to get them on.

I started stumbling back toward Mose's house. Within a mile I had a little feeling back in my feet, but my mind was working only about half speed. We continued on. We passed the fish trap. Mose did not even mention carrying it home. We finally got to Mose's house. He wanted me to come in and warm up. All my mind would function on was to go home. I loaded Ruby and started home. I drove slowly with the heater turned up all the way. I was afraid to drive at a normal rate because my mind and muscles would not work fast enough for that. By the time I got to San Marcos, I felt a little better. I stopped at Carson's and drank a bunch of coffee. I went home. I put Ruby in the pen. I went in the house and crawled in bed. I snuggled up close to Billye. She woke up and scolded me for getting so cold. She asked if I had done something stupid like falling in the river again. I told her, "Naw, I didn't fall in the river." She went back to sleep.

I lay there and shivered and thought about the hunt. I was so proud of Ruby that I could hardly contain it. I wanted to jump up and shout in glee. I wanted to tell the world what a wonderful young bitch I had. That hunt with Rachel confirmed what was in the back of my mind. I had a coonhound again. I mean a cracking, good, coonhound. I knew she was ready for whatever she encountered.

Mose White and I never hunted enough together to become close friends. In fact I never hunted with Mose again. I do not remember ever seeing him again. But do you know on this day some thirty-eight years later, I would give most of my worldly possessions to be able to go back and make that hunt with Mose and Rachel and Ruby again. Hunting don't get any better than that. Living don't either.

A Little Hunt

There was a blinding flash, and I hit the ground with a stunning jolt. Debris rained down on my head. I could hardly see, and I could hear even less. The explosion left my mind addled to the point that I was not certain I was still alive. I remembered Gus and called out to him to see if he was all right. I got no answer, but when I looked over to where he should have been I found my vision had returned enough for me to skylight him sitting flat on the ground. How did we get into this mess? Well, it all started out as good, clean, wholesome fun.

Gus Eoff and I decided that we would make a coon hunt in the area between Fentress and Lockhart, Texas, one crisp December night in the early 1960s. It is a country of mesquite and post oak, flint rocks and rolling hills, and even in winter usually sported enough rattlesnakes to keep one alert. We chose to hunt there on this night because the cold could be counted on to cut down on the number of snakes that were out and because the coons in the area had a reputation of always running well.

Gus was, in my eye, an old man at that time. He had years of experience of following hounds at night but oddly enough he had never developed any ability to navigate in the woods.

I accused him of getting lost between the steering wheel of his truck and the end gate, which in fact was only a slight exaggeration. He could train and handle hounds though, and I found the worst of his hounds to be above average. I never saw a hound that Gus owned for any time that was less than solid broke. Gus was as clean as his hounds and was truly a gentleman and a sportsman. My only quarrel with him was his use of a sputtering, stinking, flickering, old carbide light. He carried his extra carbide in an old Prince Albert can and his extra water in a half-pint whiskey bottle.

His light had the reputation of always failing when it was needed most. Gus was loyal though, even to a carbide light, and he used it up to the last night he went to the woods.

We drove into a pasture to park the truck and cast the hounds. Gus was hunting Duchess and Shotsie. I was hunting Ruby. Duchess and Shotsie were a mother-daughter team and represented something like the fourth or fifth generation of that family of grade hounds that Gus had owned. Ruby was the second generation of a family of Black and Tans I owned. As long as I am the one telling this story, I must modestly state that Ruby was the best hound we owned. So it came as no surprise to me when Ruby struck first. It was a hot track and Duchess and Shotsie were quickly both in the race. A more perfect night would be hard to imagine: a good dew, absolutely no wind, and a crisp temperature in the low 40s. It was a great night to be alive and in the woods with an old friend and good solid coonhounds.

We had a chop, a squall, and a bawl mouth represented in that pack, and the pace set by the coon soon had those rolling hills ringing with the music of the pack. This was a pack of hounds in the best sense of the term pack. They had worked together for several years. They all had about equal ability but they complemented each other in that the weakness of one hound was the strong point of another. They were honest almost to a fault and for this reason would instantly honor each other's work. They were well matched in their working speed, and this coupled with their almost blind faith in the other's work ensured that they worked as a pack and not as individuals. This combination of bitches was the best pack of coonhounds I ever followed, and they were as close to a coon catching machine as I ever saw. I knew only one other hound that could blend perfectly into this pack. He was H. A. Wallace's White Man. White Man, when added to this pack, detracted nothing and made it slightly stronger.

Let me take a moment to explain my feelings about a pack. Over the years I have seen some of the great foxhounds. The best pack of foxhounds I ever heard did not have what was considered an outstanding individual in it. They could, though, absolutely break a fox down because they ran unselfishly with each contributing to the race. I have had the pleasure, in years gone by, of seeing some of the great beagles. The best pack of beagles I ever followed did not have an outstanding individual in it. A collection of hounds does not make a pack. A individual hound can detract from the effectiveness of the group from the front, from the middle, or from behind. A fact of life is that it is difficult to put down a matched pair of any kind of hound. Three matched hounds are even harder to get together, four most difficult, and five or more are almost impossible to get together. We tend to glorify outstanding individuals, but in fact they may not fit into nor contribute much to a pack effort.

The coon we were running made a first run straight toward a dry creek and the thick brush on both sides of the creek bed. He seemed to realize that the brush did not slow the hounds any, so he tried another trick. He went up a tree and jumped out. That only slowed the pack slightly as they barked up, checked, found the track away from the tree, and continued after the coon. He then left the creek and went to a tasajillo cactus flat. He ducked and dodged in the tasajillo for a bit but even though he could get through the cactus easier than the hounds, they did not lose much ground to him. When he left the cactus flat he crossed a fresh plowed field that was to be planted in oats. The plowed field slowed the pack down and while they worked out the trail, the coon went to a dirt stock tank that held about a surface acre of water. I do not know what the coon did at that tank but it took the hounds quite some time to work out the problem he presented them. Finally they solved the puzzle and away they went. It was up to the top of a high hill, then into another tasajillo cactus patch. The pack was by this time right up on the coon, pushing him hard. He left the tasajillo and went straight back to the stock tank. Gus and I were well behind the hounds, but we could hear them working in the water. Then we heard them bay, then there was a fight, more baying, silence, then the hounds left running with the track lined out due east.

We followed the hounds at the best pace we could in the rough country. After a while the pack went out of hearing, still headed east. We went on following almost the same path used by the coon and the hounds. We crossed through a great deal of heavy post oak timbers. A large percent of those trees had hollows in them. That coon wanted no part of them. After a long period we topped a hill, and from that hilltop we could hear the hounds treeing.

The coon had gone up in an old stump of a tree. It was some ten or twelve feet high with a big hollow all the way to the ground. I climbed up and shined my light down. There he was, a huge coon with a reddish cast to his coat. I crawled back down, looked for and found a large rock of some ten or fifteen pounds. I swung the rock into the side of the dead stump with the intent of caving in the side. I jarred my hands, my arms, my body, my head and the brain within my head, but I quickly discerned that I could hardly dent the seasoned wood in that trunk. I certainly was not going to succeed in bashing it. I told Gus that it looked like that coon had made it home free.

While I was up the stump, Gus had looked the dogs over. During the fight in the tank, that big sucker had really worked our hounds over. Ruby's left eye was swollen closed. Shotsie was dripping blood from a bite through her muzzle. Poor old Duchess had been caught on the side of her tongue and a large chunk was missing from it. Gus was fighting mad. He said that we would not leave until we got that rascal out for the hounds. So, more rock swinging and banging. Then a discussion about burning him out, but both of us were afraid that we would burn up half of Central Texas if we tried that. So we had a head scratching session. I crawled back up and looked at our problem. At that moment I conceived the BIG IDEA.

"Gus," I said, "Hand me your can of carbide." I poured it in on top of the coon. "Gus," I said, "Hand me your jug of water." I poured it in on top of the carbide. I was afraid that the half pint of water was not enough, so I urinated on top of the carbide, the water and the coon. "Gus," I said, "Hand me a match."

The blinding flash, falling through the air, the sickening impact with the rocky ground, the coon staggering across my prone body, the hounds stumbling around in the chunks of wood, huge flakes of carbon floating in the air, the smell of my burned hair, Gus fumbling with his old lamp trying to get it to burn is what I remember. There was not a piece of stump left that would have been too big to burn in a small wood stove.

Gus asked if I wanted him to try to get the hounds on the trail of the coon. "Gus," I said, "You dotterin' old idiot, I am just barely alive. If it were not for the fact that you could not find the truck and, that it is at least eight miles back to a road, I would have you call an ambulance to haul me to a hospital." Gus let his bottom lip drop down a notch and mumbled something to the effect that he did not know that I was hurt. We caught up the hounds and made our way back to the truck. Gus grumbling with hurt feelings; me moaning and groaning in misery. At the truck I took inventory. All the hair was singed off the front of my head. My face was burned black. My left knee was swollen to the point that I could not bend my leg. I was sure I had a cracked rib. My eyes burned. My head hurt. My whole body ached. We made it back to town in time for a bath and breakfast before it was time to go to work. I finally finished the day—one of the longest of my life.

Billye had a good supper for me when I got in from work that night. We capped it off with mugs of hot coffee. Toward the end of the coffee, the telephone rang. It was Gus. He commented that it sure was a good night and that he knew where there was a good running coon between Staples and Kingsbury.

I hung up the phone. "Honey," I said, "I think Gus and I will make a little hunt tonight." When my wife's response came, I thought for a minute there that blammed tree had blown up again.

Rastus and Marshall

I bought Rastus from Hap Counts as a six-week-old pup. He was a registered English coonhound. His sire and dam were both from stock of the Lee Brothers who were big-game hunters in Arizona. These dogs were noted big-cat hounds. I never got to hunt with either of his parents as his sire died of heartworms and his dam was run over by a car before I ever got to the woods with them.

Rastus started easily before he was five months old. He had a beautiful bawl mouth and was almost as good a trail hound as I have ever followed. He had a good nose and he knew how to use it. He was bluetick in color and weighed about sixty pounds.

Marshall Smith was the kind of a kid that people would pick on, tease and take advantage of just because he was the kind of a kid he was. He was a good kid. He was a sweet kid. He was a quiet kid. He was shy, and finally he was a big, fat kid.

Marshall started coon hunting with me when, I would guess, he was sixteen or seventeen years old. He didn't hunt with me many times—as I can remember only three or four at the most. I do remember the last time he coon hunted with me as if it were yesterday. I took it easy on Marshall when we hunted because, as I said, he was a fat kid. He always got behind when we walked and when I would start to walk faster to the dogs treeing, he would get as much as fifty to one hundred yards behind. Never more than that but always about that much.

The last time Marshall hunted with me I took him to Preston King's ranch. It was a rocky place with lots of hills and valleys. It was covered with scrub live oak, elm, cedar, persimmon, algerita, and prickly pear and tasajillo cactus. It was joined to the north by Ed Posey, to the east by the

Lowman and Kutscher place, the south by Jess Posey, and west by Charles Rector Williams. As I remember, the King place and the ranches around would make up about five thousand acres. At that time I could hunt all this country plus another eight or ten thousand adjoining acres just as though it belonged to me.

Marshall and I progressed along on an almost routine coon hunt. We treed and shook out to the hounds several coons without getting off the King place. I had the young hound, Rastus, and Old Ruby at that time. Rastus struck a fresh track across the fence in the Kutscher place. He had not moved the track twenty-five yards before I realized that he had jumped a deer. If I was to succeed in deer-breaking Rastus, it was imperative that I catch him on this deer and castigate him severely. Just to make sure that everyone understands what my plans were, I was going to catch that dog in the act of running that deer. I was going to beat him to the point that for the rest of his life the smell of deer would make him fear for his life. My only problem was Marshall Smith. In order for me to catch Ol' Rastus, I would have to move as fast as I could and for as long a time as was required for me to run that pup down. This running would be done in rocky, hilly, brush- and cactus-infested country, and Marshall, remember, was a slow, fat kid. So, I told Marshall to stay right where he was. That I would be back for him as soon as I caught and punished Rastus. I impressed on him to stay still. That I would be back at most in an hour or two.

I took off at a pretty good pace and soon could tell that Rastus was either going to drive that deer off the Purgatory bluff on the Posey place, or he was going to swing him around to the Williams place. I heard a noise behind me, and when I looked back I saw Marshall's flashlight coming about a hundred yards back. Knowing the country I was going into, I was irritated because finding Marshall, with him moving, after I caught Rastus could prove to be a tougher job than catching Rastus. I kept moving at a steady hard trot and every time I topped a hill I would orient myself as to where Rastus was and correct my direction to intercept him. After about fifteen or twenty minutes of steady running, I looked back and much to my surprise I saw Marshall's light about a hundred yards behind me.

By this time I could tell the deer was going to go off the Purgatory Creek bluff and on to the Freeman Ranch. I wanted to catch Rastus at the bluff, if possible, so I increased my speed to the fastest I could maintain, and I held that pace for I would guess about twenty minutes until I got to the bluff. Rastus had beat me there by about a hundred yards. I really do not know how high that bluff is, but my recollection is that it is close to two hundred feet high. I never broke stride and went off that bluff in what I can only describe as a semi-controlled free fall. I got to the bottom in good shape, bolted through the boulders in the dry creek bed and opened my pace up to my top speed when I hit the flat open ground on the north side of the creek. There was a net wire fence between Posey's and Freeman's. I caught Rastus about three hundred yards from the creek at that fence. I put a lead on Rastus, stomped a limb off a cedar tree and started punishing Rastus.

About the time I finished beating Rastus, Marshall came puffing up to me. His light was broken. He had negotiated his descent down the bluff in the dark. He got to me within a few minutes after I caught Rastus. Impossible! Bear in mind that this was extremely hilly, rocky, brush country. Also keep in mind that in a period of about forty minutes we probably covered more than five miles. Also remember Marshall was a fat kid who would get behind just walking and farther behind walking fast.

The first thing I did was ask Marshall why he did not wait for me where I told him. I could not get him to answer me. We worked on his flashlight and finally got it to halfway function again. We made the hard climb up the Purgatory bluff. From the top of the bluff I could hear Ol' Ruby treeing on the King place. Marshall was about a hundred yards behind by the time I got to the tree. We held the dogs and shook the coon out and then ran him for the benefit of a freshly whipped Rastus. They caught the coon on the ground. I went to them, caught them up, and headed for my truck. Marshall was about a hundred yards behind when I got there.

Rastus never ran a deer after that. He did not make a coon dog either. He would not bark treed on a coon. He would hold the tree, but he would not bark up. A bobcat hunter from South Texas came to me and asked to buy him. I explained that he would not tree. He said he knew that, but he wanted him anyway. The cat hunter's son later told me that Rastus made a fine cat hound. That he would eat a mesquite tree up when the cat went up. I was happy. I got my money out of Rastus plus a little more. I had a good home for that money. It went to pay the hospital bill incurred when my youngest son was born.

I do not remember that Marshall ever went coon hunting with me again. Years later, after Marshall was a middle-aged man, I asked him why he had not stayed where I told him to wait for me. His answer was that he was convinced that I was going to play a prank on him and leave him in the woods, lost and alone to find his way out. The thought of that happening frightened him to the point that he took after me when I ran away from him.

In my lifetime I have seen some amazing physical accomplishments by man and beast. To this day, though, I have never seen what I consider a more remarkable feat than the one performed by that fat kid, Marshall Smith, when he was afraid of being left in the woods at night. There have been a number of times since then that I have used Marshall as an inspiration when I was faced with an almost impossible physical challenge. But for goodness sake, please do not tell Marshall that he ever served as an inspiration for me. It would ruin our whole relationship.

Breaking Jerome

Jerome Fritz walked into my store one afternoon in the winter of 1956. He introduced himself and stated that several people had told him that I was a coon hunter. He said that he had never been coon hunting and that he wanted me to take him. I answered that Gus Eoff and I were going hunting that night and that he was welcome to join us. During our conversation, I learned that he was an efficiency expert and that he was working for Johnny Hughson in his meat-packing business. Fritz looked to be about forty, was about five feet, ten inches, and probably weighed a little more than two hundred pounds. My impression was that Fritz had never done any real hard work in his whole life—soft hands, soft body, smooth conversation.

Gus and I took him hunting on the Heep Ranch between San Marcos and Wimberly. There were wild turkey feeders there and many more coons than turkeys. We probably treed ten or twelve coons and were back in town before midnight. No long races from those fed coons. Not much sport. We were just performing a service for Mr. Heep and his foreman, Eb Horner, as these coons literally ate and wasted hundreds of pounds of wild turkey feed per week.

A few days after that hunt, Fritz came by the store and told me that he had sure enjoyed the hunt and that he would like to go again. I told him fine and that I was going that night. I picked him up and took him with me to the Tom Nance Ranch on the Blanco River. We had a nice hunt, ran and treed six or eight coons, and were back home around midnight.

Fritz hunted with me a couple of nights per week for several weeks. I always took him on short hunts because I did not know how he would stand up to a hard, all-night hunt. One Sunday evening after he had made maybe a half-dozen hunts, Fritz showed up at the house and said that he would like to start hunting. That he would like to buy a coonhound already trained and did I know where he could buy one. I told Fritz that as green as he was about hounds that he was surely going to be skinned if he set out to buy a trained hound. I asked if he remembered a little bluetick bitch I had carried every time he went hunting. He replied, "Yes." I told him she was a pretty fair hound, solid broke, no bad faults, and fully capable of treeing her own coon.

Hap Counts had moved back to Fort Worth and had too many hounds to take them all with him. He gave her to me as a young, just-started pup. I caught her running a deer shortly after I got her, gave her a sound thrashing, and to my knowledge she never ran another animal other than a coon. I explained all of this to Fritz and told him he could have the bitch if he wanted her. I also explained that he would have a difficult time finding a better hound that was for sale. Fritz took the bitch.

Fritz hunted with me several nights most every week, always short hunts. Every time he showed up to go hunting, he had new equipment. A coon squaller, a leather lead, a new dog collar and name plate, a compass, a dandy flashlight, a fine German-made pocketknife, and ducking brush pants and jumper. Everything a coon hunter could need. He even took to bragging on his little bitch. Sounded just like a real coon hunter.

Suddenly winter was about over and spring was on its way. One of my favorite places in the world to run a coon is in the area of the community of Golle, close to Seguin. It was a county of rolling flint rock hills, brush covered, turned-out fields with fence rows lined with mostly hackberry, ash and elm trees, some bit of mesquite, tasajillo cactus, and lots of gullies and mostly dry creeks with an occasional hole of water in an otherwise dry creek. The coons ran better there than any I have ever seen anywhere in the U.S.A. A good pack of hounds could tree one coon there in a night. A good lucky pack might even tree two coons in a night. I was running a three-dog pack that could regularly tree two or three coons a night there. Golle coons were truly whizzes at running, and the country was so rough that it gave the coon the advantage. The only drawback to hunting the Golle county was its supply of rattlesnakes. They were thick. Consequently, I mostly only hunted there in the dead of winter in order to protect the hounds. Since winter was about over, I wanted to enjoy one last, good hunt there before the coming of spring and its rattlesnakes. Fritz said he wanted to go hunting there with me.

I parked my truck on a county dirt road at the top of a big hill on a Saturday night. This hill sloped down north for almost a mile to a creek bed. There was a big oat patch between the road and the dry creek bed. We unloaded the hounds—Ruby, Honeybunch, Rastus, and Fritz's little bitch—and walked down toward the creek. The hounds struck in the creek bed before Fritz and I got out of the oat patch. The coon headed out going mostly east and north. We took in after them making the best time we could, but believe me that between the big loose flint rocks underfoot and the brush and tasajillo cactus and the hills, we were not setting any speed records. After a bit I noticed that Fritz was having a difficult time keeping up. He even asked how he would get out of there if he got lost from me. I told him not to worry that I would find him in the morning. I noticed Fritz kept up a lot better after that.

After a couple of hours we topped a hill, and I could hear Ol' Ruby treeing to the north. We finally got to the tree and the hounds had us a dandy nice big coon up a big live oak, down in a creek bed. We shook him out and the hounds stretched him just slick as could be. I hung the dead coon up in a fork of the tree and before I could start walking back toward the truck, the hounds started another coon. This one also ran mostly east and north. We fought the rocks, cactus, and hills, but it was sure hard to try to stay in hearing of the hounds. Several times I heard the hounds bark up, but each time the coon would travel through the treetops on a fence line and come down running. Ol' Ruby was too smart to get left holding an empty tree, but the coon would usually gain some time on the hounds before she figured it out.

About this time Fritz asked me if I knew where he could get a drink of water. I explained that there were no faucets in this part of the world and that we could get a drink when we got back to town. At what I judged to be about two o'clock, it started to fog in on us, at least it was foggy down in the low places. The high ground was clear as a bell. Finally we treed the second coon. I could not climb that tree. It wasn't too bad a tree. I am just a miserable tree climber. Fritz said he did not want to climb the tree, so we caught and led the dogs off.

The dogs started the third coon while they were still on the leads. I cut them aloose and the race was on. I was glad to note that this coon was running in at least a general direction back toward the truck. Fritz asked me not to go off and leave him and by this time he had really slowed down. So we followed the hounds at a much slower pace. Finally just as day was first breaking, I heard the dogs settle in solid on a tree. When we got there, we found a big hollow in an old live oak down in a creek bed. We called off the hounds, and I told Fritz that we would follow the creek for about a mile. Then we would be at the oat patch.

When I got to the oat patch, I had to wait for Fritz. He finally caught up, and I asked him if he was all right. He said that other than two sprained ankles from walking on flint rocks, cactus thorns all in his legs, a case of dehydration and extreme fatigue, he thought he was okay. I told him to cheer up as it was only about a mile up the hill through the easy walking of the oat patch to the truck. When I got there, I loaded my hounds and looked back down the hill. All the lower half of that valley was covered in fog. I sat on the end gate of the truck and watched for a long time before Fritz came plodding out of the fog. After an even longer time he finally made it to the truck. I loaded his hound. He never said a word . . . just got in the truck. He also had nothing to say during the fifteen-mile drive to his house. At his house I unloaded his hound and handed him the lead. He still said nothing. As I left to go home, he was still standing there holding his dog.

Monday night, as I worked on a blowing horn, I heard my hounds barking in the pen. Shortly after that there was a knock on the door. It was Fritz. He had a big sack in his hand. He said he had put the bluetick bitch back in my pen and that he had quit hunting. He said he wanted to give me all of the hunting gear he had accumulated: the lead, the flashlight, the knife, the jumper, the whole works. I thanked him for the presents and asked him why he was quitting. He replied that the Saturday night's hunt had left him completely exhausted and that he had not recovered enough to be able to go to work on

Monday morning. I apologized for hunting him that hard and stated that I did not realize that we were hunting hard enough to hurt him. He said he understood that, and he said he had a favor to ask me. His favor was that he wanted the hunting horn I was working on as a souvenir to remember his coon-hunting days, which he stated, were the happiest of his life. I gave him the horn a few days later as soon as I finished it, having worked it into a really fine example of a blowing horn.

In the days and weeks after Fritz quit hunting I gave it a lot of thought. I wondered what kind of a life Fritz had led for a couple of months of coon hunting to have been the happiest time of his life. I tried to look inside myself to determine if I had been deliberately cruel to him. In an effort to make amends I went by and invited him to go hunting several times. He always answered that I would never know what the warm friendship and camaraderie expressed in our hunts meant to him, but that he would not hunt again.

He said, "Taylor, remember telling me how you broke the little bluetick bitch from running off game? Well Taylor, you broke me from coon hunting by thrashing me with a good, hard, all-night hunt. And, Taylor, like the little bluetick bitch—I am solid broke!"

I have not seen Fritz in more than thirty years. Haven't thought of him in probably twenty-five. Sure hope that man found something that made him happier than getting broke from running coons.

The Climber

Oscar Strahn retired as athletic director of Southwest Texas State University in the early 1960s. I think the inactivity of retired life was getting to him. As a result he came by the store and asked to go coon hunting with me one fall day, as I remember, in 1962. I took him to the Freeman Ranch and turned aloose a dandy three-dog pack of solid coonhounds. At that time those hounds would average treeing a coon every twenty minutes. I told Mr. Strahn to holler when he had enough, and I would catch up the hounds and go. Well, at daylight the next morning I told Mr. Strahn that I had to open the store at 7:30, so we needed to go. What I am trying to say is that the old man loved to coon hunt, and he would stay with you. He hunted with me quite a few nights that winter. Good hunt or bad, he always seemed to enjoy himself. As we got to know each other, we learned that we both enjoyed playing chess. As a result we starting playing chess one night a week from eight in the evening until I had to open the store at 7:30 the next morning. We had some delightful battles on the chess board.

One night before we started our chess game, he asked if I ever had ankle or knee problems relating to hunting in the rough-hill country. My answer was that before I moved to San Marcos and started hunting the hill country, I had both weak ankles and weak knees. That after a couple of years of hunting in the rocky, rough country much of the time with no light in order to conserve batteries, my knees never bothered me. My ankles were so strong that nothing I could do would cause a sprain. He told me that his interest was because the university was having a rash of ankle and knee injuries in their athletes. He had reached the conclusion that hunting with me under my conditions would strengthen both ankles and knees. He wanted to know if my experience bore that out. He next asked if he could send a couple of recovering injured athletes to hunt with me to see what effect it would have on their legs. It was all right with me.

In a few days one of the athletes showed up at the store wanting to know when we were going hunting. He was huge—tall and broad. I did not notice any baby fat on him either.

We hunted from my house on a Saturday night. I cast the hounds down toward Purgatory Creek, which in those days was a horror of huge jumbled rocks, brush, and cactus. I explained to the football player what to expect on a coon hunt, my responsibilities, and the dog's responsibilities. Mr. Football Player did not show even polite interest. The hounds struck, and after a fast and furious race they nailed the coon up a medium-sized elm tree. I explained that I was a miserable tree climber and that I would appreciate it if he would climb up the tree and shake out the coon. Mr. Football Player stated that he could climb.

The coon was a big one and in the top of the tree. When the Climber got almost to the coon, he asked what to do. I instructed him to shake the limb, and that would cause the coon to jump. He did and the coon did. The dogs caught the coon as it hit the ground. The coon put up a spirited fight, partly because of its size and partly because my dogs were not good kill dogs. Good kill dogs in my experience are dogs that have seen only a limited number of coons. Dogs that look at ten or more coons a night for at least three nights a week and some fifty weeks a year have a tendency after a while to get a little shy in a fight. I have seen a few exceptions to this but not many. Anyway my Climber seemed to enjoy the fight, but he stated that he thought my dogs lacked real courage.

The next coon was started in short order, and this one went up a good-sized live oak tree. The Climber went up to the coon, who was on the outer part of a small limb but turned back facing the Climber. The Climber asked how to get this coon out. I instructed him to take his cap and slap the coon in the face with it, which would cause the coon to jump. He did and the coon did and another slam bang street brawl followed when the coon hit the ground. As we left the tree, the Climber stated that if he were a coon hunter, he would not keep hounds that were as cowardly as mine.

The next coon was treed in a nice-sized cedar (juniper) tree. My Climber only had to climb up with his feet just over head high to get at the coon, which was on a small limb with his head facing the stars. He asked how to get this one out, and this time I told him to grab the tip of its tail and pitch it down. He did, and since this was a medium-sized coon the hounds stretched it instantly. My remark about my hounds quickly killing this one was answered by a reply to the effect that even baby puppies should be able to handle baby coons.

When Ol' Ruby struck the next coon, she must have run up on it face to face. Almost before Black and Blunder could bark, she had it treed. The tree, when we got to it, was one with a hollow in it. I looked the tree over and remarked that the coon was in the hollow, which was at the end of a big five- or six-foot limb that had been cut off years before. The Climber went up, stretched out on the limb, looked in, said the coon was there, and asked how to get him out.

The mean streak my Momma always said I had rose to the surface at that moment. I innocently answered for him to reach in, grab the coon by the scuff of his neck, pull him out, and toss him to the hounds. He did—reach in and grab the coon that is. You know that ol' boy forgot how to turn a coon aloose. Amid a frantic human scream and curdling coon squall, both Climber and coon came flailing out of the tree. The Climber was in a flying nose dive with the coon rolled up around his left forearm. Sounded like a watermelon had hit the ground when the Climber's head hit. The dogs were on the coon in an instant.

That football-playing young man was one tough fellow because he let out a roar, shook his head, and got up on his hands and knees. The coon, fighting valiantly, worked his way under the protection of the Climber's body. Every time the Climber would start to get the rest of the way up, a dog would lunge at the coon. The combination of the actions of a sixty-five-pound dog, a sixty-pound dog, a forty-five-pound dog, and a fifteen-pound coon kept my Climber off balance to the point he could not get up off his hands and knees.

I stood there for a while, fascinated while I watched the action. Finally I decided to grab the coon's tail and pitch it out into the open so the dogs would have clean access to it. Just as I started in, I saw Black slip in between the Climber's legs and grab the coon by the tail end. The coon tried to roll up Black's head, but it succeeded only in rolling up into the crotch of my Climber. Funny thing, but that young fellow got right up on his feet then with no help from me at all. This action allowed the coon to get at Black's head, which it did with great relish. Blunder slipped around and got a clean shot at the coon's throat. With Blunder in a choke hold, Black stretched the coon, and Ruby crushed its chest. They quickly had him dead, neat as a pin.

I shined my light on my Climber. He was a wreck—bloody face, bloody hands, and hunched over holding his crotch. Ol' Ruby slipped off during this time and started another coon. Black and Blunder soon put in, and after a short run this coon went up a tree between us and my house. I asked my Climber if he could make it. He indicated he could, so we set out for the house by way of the treed coon. Turned out to be a hollow tree. I asked the Climber if he would like to go up and pull this one out of the hollow for the dogs. He declined my offer. I climbed to the hollow, which was big around and shallow. I reached in, grabbed the coon by the tail and jerked him up with all the quickness I had. As he cleared the hollow I let go and the coon fell right in the middle of the dogs. After another good fight, they stretched him.

On the way home, I kind of came down hard on the Climber because he had quit getting coons out of the trees after only four attempts. I explained that getting the coons out was the easy part. The hard part was in killing the coon. I explained that Ol' Ruby had probably been in on the kill of over 10,000 coons and that Black and Blunder had fought over 2,000. Since he had criticized them for being a little shy of the tooth end of a coon, I thought he owed them an apology since he had completely quit after only four coons. Ol' Climber did not respond in any way. When we got to the house, he refused my offer of first aid, even though his ring finger was badly swollen from a coon bite and the ring was still on the finger. Made me feel bad to look at it. He got in his truck and left. You know, he never came back for more knee rehabilitation.

Twenty years later I was in a fertilizer plant in Floresville, Texas. A big fellow with hair all over his face was there at the plant. He kept looking at me and after a while he told me who I was. I told him I sure did not recognize him. He said he was Charley Fuller. I did not remember a Charley Fuller. He said I had taken him coon hunting one time. I replied that I took hundreds of people hunting. He said Oscar Strahn had arranged the hunt. "I'll be damn," I said, "You are the Climber!"

Ol' Charley and I had a good, long visit. Seems that he had cat and coonhounds. Told me straight out that they could not kill coons from shucks. Would bet that Charley made a pretty good hunter and that he had a pack of good dogs. Would also bet he had learned how to turn a coon aloose when he had it in his hands.

You never can tell. He might have even gotten smart enough to keep his hands off them old bad coons.

Dr. Scheib and Ruby

I was up in the tree looking down at Ruby, Black, and Blunder fighting the coon I had just jumped out on them. I am colorblind, but as I looked down I could see that something was terribly wrong. It looked as though there were dog parts scattered all around the dogs fighting the coon. I jumped down, slammed my foot down on the throat of the huge boar coon, and jammed my opened pocketknife into his rib cage. In a matter of seconds he was dead.

I grabbed Ol' Ruby as the two young hounds continued to maul the dead coon. The hide on the underside of her belly was ripped open in a big V that extended from between her front legs all the way back to past her last teats. Her intestines trailed out all over the ground. With her on her back, I gathered up her intestines and crammed them back into her body cavity. They were all covered with dirt, sticks, and leaves. I ripped off the bottom half of my shirt and tied it around her body to hold in her insides. I necked the two young dogs together, and as I gathered Ruby up in my arms, I called them and headed to the truck.

I got into this nightmare because I was angry with a coon. The Thursday night before this awful Saturday night, I had taken the young hounds, Black and Blunder, hunting. They were about twelve months old, and I had noticed that they were depending too much on their mother, Ruby, to locate for them. I left Ruby home so that they would be forced to depend on their own ability to locate the coon.

I cast them from the old caliche pit on Preston King's place. I hunted them toward the dirt tank on the southeast corner of the place.

They struck, and I can assure you that starting, trailing, jumping, and running a coon was not their weakness. They quickly had that coon jumped and running. Blunder had a big booming bawl mouth, while Black had a blistering coarse chop. The race progressed at a furious pace for almost three-quarters of an hour, and then there was nothing but a long silence.

Finally Black located and tentatively barked up. Blunder honored him, and in a short time it sounded as if they were going to eat that tree up. They were in the Kutscher place, but the tree they were barking up was only a couple of hundred yards from where they had originally started the coon. That old coon had run a long race but treed close to where he had been started.

I caught his eye in the top of a cedar (juniper) tree long before I got to the tree. He was a big coon by Texas hill-country standards, and my guess was that he would have weighed close to fifteen pounds. The cedar tree was easy to climb, and he jumped out before I had gotten halfway to him. I backed down to watch the fight. He was backed up in a algerita brush, and Blunder was baying him straight on, face to face. Black eased to one side and made a grab at his throat. That boar grabbed Black as he came in and rolled up on his head. Black changed direction and ran backward for quite a distance. Blunder then caught up and grabbed the coon in the lower part of his back. The coon turned Black aloose and locked up on Blunder's head. The action continued for a long time, least that is the way it seemed to me. Part of the time the dogs would bay the coon. Then as the coon would start to move away, one of them would grab him, only to have his head worked over. I began to notice that the coon was working back to the King place.

He finally worked his way to the double net-wire fence between the two places. The fence held the dogs up a bit, at which point the coon broke and ran. The dogs caught him right on the edge of the dirt tank, and by the time I got there, he had taken the dogs into the water and had Black drowned down. That coon was in the process of putting Blunder's head under every time he came up.

I had no choice, so in I went clothes, billfold, boots, and all. I got Black out first, then Blunder. The coon left, and by the time I got both hounds on their feet I could tell they had all the coon hunting they wanted for that night. I was furious with that coon for having beaten up my young hounds.

That Saturday night I loaded up all three of my dogs and went back to the King place. As luck would have it, we started that big rascal very close to where he was started the Thursday before. He ran the same kind of a race and treed within fifty yards of where he treed before. I heard Ol' Ruby bark funny as she crossed the net wire fence into the Kutscher place, but I really did not think anything of it. As I approached the tree with all three dogs treeing, I caught its eye. The coon was in the top of a small live oak tree. I kept my light on it as I climbed up to shake it out. When I looked down, I first discovered that something was wrong with Ruby.

I went by Doc Tickle's house as soon as I got into town. No one was home. I went home and called the vet at New Braunfels—no answer. I tried to reach two veterinarians in Seguin with no success. Then a couple in Austin. There did not seem to be a vet available to me anywhere in my part of the world that Saturday night.

The rest of that night we spent sitting up with the injured dog. She had a glazed look in her eye that frightened me, but she sure did not complain any. The next morning I continued my efforts to locate a vet, but I again met with no success. As the morning wore on, I was in a state of extreme mental anguish over my inability to get any help for Ruby.

Just before noon Billye suggested that I ask our family doctor, Dr. William Scheib, for his help. At that point I would have accepted help from anyone. I called Dr. Scheib. He told me to meet him at his office and that he would do what he could.

Dr. Scheib was a crooked, twisted gnome of a man. He was one of the kindest, most gentle persons I have ever known. It was my understanding that he moved to San Marcos, away from his regular practice in one of the northern states, because of problems with his health.

He was waiting for me at his office when I got there. When he saw how serious the injuries were he stated that he did not think he could help Ruby because the operation would require an anesthetic, and he knew nothing about anesthetizing a dog. He said he was sure that the improper use of anesthetic would kill her. I knew Ol' Ruby as well as I knew myself. I told him to go ahead with the operation. That Ruby and I would handle the anesthetic.

We laid her out on the table. I talked to her the whole time as Dr. Scheib got her ready. I told her, "Old Lady, we are going to hurt you, but it has to be done. Your job will be to lay there and take it without moving." Then I commanded her loudly, "Hold still Old Lady! Hold Still!"

Dr. Scheib cleaned her insides of all the dirt, sticks, trash, and leaves that he could. He then started sewing her up. He worked on that bitch for a little over three hours. Ruby flinched one time about two hours into the operation. I scolded her, "Hang on Old Lady! Hold Still!" She never moved again. Finally he had done all he could do for her, and it was time for us to leave.

I said, "Doc, what do I owe you?" He answered, "Mr. Taylor, if you promise not to let word get back to any of the local doctors about me operating on a dog, then you owe me nothing." Then he said, "Sometime I get the feeling that they think I am just an old veterinarian anyway, so let's not confirm their thoughts by broadcasting that I did operate on a dog." I gave him my thanks, and as I turned to leave he stated that he liked to eat coon and that I just might leave a fat young coon carcass at his house sometime.

I cast Black and Blunder from the house as soon as I had made Ruby comfortable. The second coon they treed was a nice, young, fat one. I had it dressed and handed it to Dr. Scheib before it was good and dark. Several times a year until Dr. Scheib died, I would dress a coon for him. As I started to leave, Dr. Scheib told me that I had the most remarkable control over my dog that he had ever seen. He said that it did not seem possible that I could, by voice command alone, make her hold still through all the pain he had inflicted on her.

My answer to this was that I doubted that I had any real control over the bitch; she was far too hardheaded for that. I felt what he had seen was a feeling of trust and confidence that Ruby and I shared. My absolute trust and confidence that she gave me her very best every time I put her down and her unswerving trust and confidence that I would do my best for her every time she needed me.

She was five years old when this happened. Thanks to Dr. Scheib she had almost nine more years ahead of her. That wonderful old man never knew how much he enriched my life by saving Ruby for me.

Think for a moment what an absolute game hound Ruby was. She ripped herself open getting through the net wire fence. She ran the coon more than a hundred yards to the tree with her intestines trailing out on the ground. She treed with her front feet on the tree as she poured out her ringing chop tree mouth. She fought the coon with her insides scattered all over the ground. Son, Ruby was one tough coonhound.

There is another thing I would like for you to consider. There is a public building in San Marcos, Texas, that is dedicated to helping handicapped people. It is named after Dr. Scheib and is called the Scheib Center. There was a wagonload of doctors in San Marcos at the time Dr. Scheib sewed Ruby up for me. All of them are either dead or retired now. Funny thing, they may have made snide remarks about Dr. Scheib behind his back, and some of them did because I heard them. Be that as it may, there is nothing dedicated to any of them in this world to honor them for the good work they have done. Little, old, crippled Dr. Scheib was simply one hell of a man.

Gus the Killer and Friday Ellis

Friday Lee Ellis was a rodeo performer and also a rodeo clown back in the 1930s and 1940s. During the twenty-odd years I knew him, he made part of his living working cattle for other people, and he was especially good at catching and handling bad, wild cattle. Another part of his living was derived from raising, selling, and fighting game chickens. When the chips were down and Friday was flat broke, you could depend on him loading up some of his fighting cocks and making a big cock fight. You could almost automatically depend on him to come out with first-place money. The rest of his income came from selling hides from coons and ringtails he trapped, headlighted, or treed in fur season. Friday did not hunt for sport, so therefore he did not want a trailing hound. He mostly used a treeing cur-dog.

Just for those of you who may not know, a ringtail is a ringtail cat. It is a small nocturnal animal about twice the size of a fox squirrel. It has a ringed tail like a coon and has huge eyes. He spends a good portion of his life up in trees, and he will eat almost anything from berries to insects to birds. Ringtails are quite plentiful in the hill country of Texas. During the time I knew Friday, coon hides brought fifty cents and ringtails a dollar and a half.

One day Friday stopped by the store and told me he had a hound he wanted me to see. I think he said he got the dog from the Eastwoods. The dog was a big, stoutly built Black and Tan that showed a touch of cur in him. Friday emphasized that the dog was a "coon-killing machine." I really did not want the dog, but that "coon killing machine" tickled a little part of my brain that stored deflated egos and hurt pride. I explained to Friday that I did not want the dog but that I would sure like to see him kill a few coons. The fur season was over, and Friday welcomed the idea of me feeding his dog for a while.

I once went to a coon meet that was held by a creek just off the Old Manor Road out of Austin, Texas. Now this meet was strictly a contest for entertainment, using unnatural conditions to show some coon-dog abilities. Another type of coon-dog contest was a night hunt, where wild coons were run under natural conditions so a hound could compete with other hounds to demonstrate its ability to start, trail, and tree coons. Anyway, they had a number of contests to entertain us: coon treeing, coon on a log, coon in a hole, and coon in a log. For the purposes of this tale I will only describe the coon in a log contest.

The "log" was constructed of heavy two-inch-thick lumber that was, as I remember, twelve- or fourteen-inches high and also the same width. I remember the "log" as some six- or eight-feet long. It had two sides, a top and a back. The front was open and the bottom was the bare ground. Anyone who wished could enter his dog in any event. At that meet, the entry fee was five dollars. Entry money went in a pot, and it was winner-take-all. The entered dogs were drawn by lot. A heavy cord was tied around the waist of a big, freshly caught, wild coon. The cord was threaded through a small hole in the back of the log and the coon was pulled all the way up snug against the back of the log. A line was drawn some six feet in front of the log. The handler of the dog would take his dog up to the front of the log and let the dog smell and see the coon. Then he would drag the dog back to the line. The timekeeper would slap the handler on the shoulder and start his stopwatch. The handler would release the dog, whose job was then to go in the log and bring the coon out. When the coon cleared the log, the timekeeper stopped the stopwatch. The quickest time for the event was the winner. The log was small enough to really crowd a dog. It was also small enough that the dog could only get at the business end of the coon. If there were fifteen dogs entered, it would have been a safe bet that less than five dogs would bring the coon out of the log. If a coon were injured during this process, a fresh coon replaced it.

I had with me at this meet the best coonhound I have ever followed, Taylor's Black Ruby. A number of my buddies egged me to enter her. It did not take much encouragement as I sure had a use for that prize money. It happened that I was drawn as one of the last contestants, so I watched the competition closely. The dogs would really raise a ruckus when they were shown the coon. They would lunge at the lead in an effort to get at the coon. But no matter how hyped up the dog was, few were able to bring the coon out of the log. Finally my time came. I led Ruby up to the log. She looked in the log. I took her back to the starting line. The timer slapped my shoulder. I turned her aloose. She walked around me away from the log and its coon, laid down under my truck, curled up in a ball, and went to sleep. And that was the end of that. That bitch may have been a coon-starting, coon-running, coon-treeing wonder, but she would have no part of a caught, tied coon. The whole gathering exploded in roaring humiliating laughter. I was teased unmercifully by friends and strangers alike. So now you know why I had the little smoldering spot in my brain that houses deflated egos and hurt pride.

I took the dog from Friday and since I had not asked his name, I called him Gus just to agitate my old hunting partner, Gus Eoff. Well, Gus was a coon killer. After my hounds treed a coon, I would tie them off and shake the coon out on Gus. When the coon jumped from the tree, Gus got to where he would meet the coon six or eight feet up in the air. He would have it crushed and shook to death by the time he got back to the ground. Big coon or little, dry land or water, Gus did his thing—he killed coons. He just inhaled them all wherever they were. *Whee doggies*! After watching that killer for about thirty coons worth, I went a looking for a coon meet.

Well, I found one for the next Sunday at the same spot where the one I had first been to was held. Ol' Gus, the killer, and I got there early. On the way there I got to figuring just how much money we could win. I thought maybe eighty dollars for the coon on a log, seventy dollars for the coon in a hole, and maybe even a hundred dollars for the coon in a log. All together two-hundred-and-fifty dollars!

They had the coon in a log contest first. I could not plunk my entry money down fast enough. Hot damn! More than twenty dogs entered. Why me and Ol' Gus were going to make a bunch more than a hundred dollars on this first event. Shoot man! It looked like we were going to come out with more than three hundred dollars out of three events. They held the drawing, and Gus was drawn third. I watched the first two dogs. Both of these two dogs came backing out of the log faster than they went in. Neither could face up to the coon in such cramped quarters. This was going to be easier than I thought!

I got Gus and led him up to the log. When that killer saw and smelled that coon he went into a raging fit. Now Gus was a big dog of maybe eighty pounds. He was as hard as a rock and big and powerful. I was not able to pull him back to the starting line by myself because he was stronger than I was. I got a couple of bystanders to help me. I yelled over all the noise Gus was making to the man holding the cord that held the coon to the back of the log. I told him to be sure to release the cord when Gus hit the coon so Gus could remove the coon from the log.

I had run an unknotted rope through Gus's collar and doubled it back. That way all I had to do was release one end of the rope and Gus was free to go to work. I had the two bystanders hold my belt from behind to keep Gus from jerking me across the starting line. The starter slapped my shoulder. I turned aloose one end of the rope. Gus hit that log so hard he almost knocked the coon-holding man off his feet at the back of the log. I am sure I saw that log bulge as Gus slammed in after the coon. I had never heard such a roar as I heard from Gus in the log. Then I could see him coming out. Hot damn! Money in the bank.

All of a sudden I realized something was wrong. Gus's roar had turned into a yipping of fear. Gus came out of that log headfirst. Uh-Oh! There was just no way that big sucker could have turned around in the close confines of that log! When Gus cleared that log I saw that the coon-holding man had done his job because that coon was aloose and riding on Gus's rump and a chewing like he had something good to eat.

Gus's mouth was open wide enough that a person could have thrown a loaf of bread down it. His eyes were wide open with terror and bulging from his head. Gus went through the crowd bowling over people like matchsticks, all the while giving his bloody murder yelp. An old man at the edge of the crowd told me that the last he could see of them, the coon was still a riding him and spurring him every jump. He said the dog was still gaining speed as he went out of sight in the weeds of an open field.

Took over an hour for me to find Ol' Gus. You talk about a hangdog look. When I found him, he was quivering like he was made of Jell-O. I eased up to my truck, loaded the dog, and slipped away. I was in no mood to take the joshing of the crowd. I expect I had a hangdog look too. All the way home I recounted all the money Gus failed to win.

Monday, after work, I took Gus back to Friday. I thanked him for letting me look at his dog. Then as quickly as I could, I put the memory of that dog in the part of my brain that holds hurt pride and deflated egos. Then I just turned that part of my brain plumb off.

The next winter, the day after fur season opened, Friday came to the store. He asked what I had done to his dog. He explained that the old dog would not even get close to a coon, much less kill one. What could I do? I told him the whole story. I stated that since I had ruined his dog I wanted to pay for him. Now Friday Lee Ellis and I were friends. He was a good man and a square-shooter. He told me the Eastwoods had given him the dog because he was not fit for anything but killing coons. He said he and I started out even and that we were still even.

Friday died, as I remember, in the mid-1970s. I will bet he left this world on even terms with everyone in it. He never knew anything but hard times and hard work his whole life. He left behind a wife, who was as fine a lady as I have ever known. He also left two daughters I do not know, but I will bet they are good people, too. I am sure enough to bet on them because I know their pedigree.

Nickel Plated and Pearl Handled

One Saturday night in the fall of 1961, Red Wallace came over from San Antonio to go coon hunting with me. I took him to the Freeman Ranch to hunt. Rufus Alexander was foreman of the ranch at that time, and his house was located on the Wimberly highway. Fernando Trinidad had worked on the Freeman Ranch for many years, and he lived at what was called Headquarters, which was located off a county road several miles from the Wimberly highway. I had known Fernando pretty well for about seven years. I had permission to hunt this ranch anytime I wanted, any way I wanted. As I remember, the Freeman Ranch was made up of six- or eight-thousand acres.

My plan was to take Red to some country northeast of Headquarters where there were good running coons and plenty of them. As we drove past the big two-story house where Fernando lived, I noticed there were no lights, and no one appeared to be at home. When we got to the gate that would let us drive through the cattle-working pens into the pasture I wanted to hunt, I was surprised to find a truckload of gravel dumped in front of the gate so the gate would not open. I told Red that was all right. We would just park there, cast the hounds, and hunt away from Headquarters afoot.

As I remember we had a good hunt and treed and killed a good number of coons. I was hunting my Ruby bitch while Red was hunting his White Man. Those two hounds were about as good as coonhounds get. We each had a young hound with us that night to work with the old dogs. I started in a direction that was east from Headquarters, and as we hunted along I worked us in a big loop so that we would end up back at Headquarters where we had left the truck.

Red's wife, Madeline, had come with him that night. Madeline stayed at my house to visit with Billye while we hunted. Along about midnight Red said he thought it would be a good idea to catch up the dogs and go in as he would catch a little flack from Madeline if he stayed out too late. I caught my two dogs but Red was only able to catch White Man. Red said that was all right as he was sure his pup would come in when he discovered there were no dogs aloose with him.

Just as we got to the pens, we heard his pup strike a coon in a draw about three-fourths of a mile from us. Red started sputtering about his luck in having to go back after the pup. I told Red that if he could lift the gate off its hinges and set it out of the way, I thought I could get my pickup over the mound of gravel. I told him the pup was working in a direction that would cross a road we could get to easily. We loaded the dogs, Red moved the gate, and I jumped my little gray Ford pickup over the pile of gravel. Just as we got to the draw the pup was working, we saw the pup cross the road ahead of us in the truck's headlights. As I got to the spot the pup crossed, Red jumped out and ran after the pup. It was a pretty warm night and Red was a little overweight, so it took him several hundred yards to catch the pup. When he got back to the truck and loaded the pup, he said he was sure thirsty and hadn't we passed a windmill where he could get a drink? I told him we had passed a windmill all right but that the water from it was unfit for humans. I explained that it was really bad-tasting water and that it would flush you like Epsom salts.

At that moment I heard a truck coming toward us from the direction of Headquarters and that truck was going so fast it was only hitting the high spots. I told Red that it had to be Fernando and that he had to be excited about something. Since Red was a stranger to Fernando I suggested that he step behind a big oak tree that was fifteen or twenty yards off the road so I could face Fernando alone.

Red had hardly gotten behind the tree when the pickup started down into the draw we were in. They were going so fast they hit their brakes and slid on the loose caliche road almost up to the back of my truck. I was standing there with their headlights full on me.

Fernando jumped out of the passenger side of the truck and a young man jumped out of the driver's side. Fernando ran up to me and jammed a cocked, nickel-plated, pearl-handled, Smith & Wesson .38 Special pistol in my belly. The driver put a cocked Model 94 Winchester .30-30 rifle to my head. I recognized the driver as Fernando's son-in-law.

I said, "Fernando! Damn Man! Don't you know who I am?" Both men were so agitated and disturbed that they were understanding no English that night. I switched to my best Spanish and either my Spanish failed me or they were understanding no Spanish that night either. I could not make them realize who I was and they jabbered things at me I sure did not understand.

In the late 1950s and early 1960s I was doing a good deal of competitive pistol shooting. In those days one never saw a Smith & Wesson pistol with a sorry trigger pull. They all had light, crisp, clean triggers. I thought about the nervous hand holding that cocked Smith & Wesson pistol in my belly and the light trigger pull it must have. I could feel the muscles of my belly trying to crawl out of the way of the gun barrel and the bullet I expected from it. I remember thinking that if I had to get shot why did it have to be by a nickel-plated, pearl-handled pistol or a .30-30 rifle. The pearl-handled, nickel-plated pistol was a combination any target pistol shooter would hold in disdain in 1961. The lever action rifle of .30-30 caliber is one that any real rifle nut would hold in mild contempt also.

I talked fast. I talked slow. I talked soft. I screamed. I talked English. I talked Spanish. Fernando and his son-in-law were talking too. They talked fast and they talked loud. They never understood a word I said. I never understood a word they said. Terror and fear settled in around us and were so pervasive that they almost seemed to have physical characteristics. I saw my situation as hopeless and that I had to do something.

I reached down and slipped my left hand over the pistol in such a way that I had the web of my thumb blocking the fall of the hammer as I gripped the cylinder and frame of the gun. At the same time I reached up with my right hand and I grabbed the rifle barrel just back of the muzzle. This gave me superior leverage, and I pushed the barrel away from my temple and up into the air. As I started to twist the pistol to break Fernando's grip from it, the young son-in-law hollered. "I know you, you are from the feed store." Both men turned loose of their guns. I told Fernando, "Dammit, go to the house and if anyone as much as looks out the window as I leave I will shoot them." I also told him that I would return the guns some time later. They got in their truck and left.

Red came out from behind the tree. I asked Red what he would have done if they had shot me. Red stammered he did not think he could do anything except stand behind the tree and shake. We both laughed.

I suddenly realized my mouth was as dry as it had ever been in my life. I had to have a drink of water. I drove up to the windmill with the bad water, and I drank a bunch of it. Funny thing, at that moment it tasted pretty good, and it did not bother by digestive system at all. Could be that a full dose of fear and a big charge of adrenaline overcame the bad taste and flushing effect of that water. Who knows?

I returned the guns the next day. I asked Fernando what had disturbed him so much that he reacted the way he did. His answer was that both he and his son-in-law had been to a dance that night and that they had both consumed a number of beers. He said years before as he came in one night he saw a light in the pasture. He went to investigate and found two men loading goats in a truck. They told him Joe Freeman had sent them to get the goats. Fernando helped them load the goats. It turned out the men were stealing the goats. Joe Freeman chewed Fernando out about this for months. He promised Fernando that if it ever happened again, Fernando was fired. Fernando told me he was convinced that I was there to steal goats.

Twenty-four years later I had my home in San Marcos up for sale so I could build my present home on my place close to Edna. A lady stopped by and asked to see the house. She was looking for a house for her single-parent daughter. I told her to work through the realtor. In a few days everything had been arranged to close the deal.

Joe and Ofelia Vasquez were the parents of the single-parent girl. Joe and Ofelia, Billye and I, plus most of the vultures needed to close a real estate deal were sitting around a table. We were waiting for one more vulture. It got pretty quiet during the wait, so to relieve the tension I started a conversation. I told Joe that he looked familiar to me and asked if he recognized me. He replied, "No." I asked about his parents. No one I knew there. I asked Ofelia about her parents. She said her father was Fernando Trinidad.

I turned to Joe and asked, "Joe, do you remember trying to kill me?" I could almost see the pieces of the puzzle fall in place in Joe's mind as a startled look came to his face.

He said, "Taylor, you still want to sell this house?"

Coon hunting is one thing, a .30-30 rifle is another thing. Neither of them have any bearing on a real-estate deal, so I said, "Sure Joe, I can't think of anyone I would rather sell to."

Fernando Trinidad died a fairly old man, as I remember, in the mid 1970s. Joe Vasquez died as a young man in about 1986 or 1987. Fernando Trinidad was considered as an honest, hardworking, good man. He was deeply respected by all who knew him well. I would bet Joe Vasquez was too. I do not remember them because they were good men, though. I remember them because on a fall night in 1961 they were the reason that some of the worst well water in Texas tasted awfully good to me.

Two Batches of Ticks

Somewhere around 1963 a man came to visit me from Utah. The object of his visit was to buy some of my Black and Tan hounds. I think the man's name was Yarrington. The funny part was that I told him before he came that I did not have any hounds for sale. Anyway I am pretty sure he came in early summer of 1963.

When he arrived in San Marcos, he came to the house and looked at my hounds. He wanted to go hunting that night. I took him up on the Freeman Ranch, and my pack put on a show for him. Several times during the hunt he would offer me money for my dogs. About one o'clock he said that his wife was alone in the motel, and he was afraid she would be uneasy by herself. He asked me to take him back to the motel. I left the pack running and took him. On the way he offered to trade me his new Ford pickup truck for three of my hounds. I told him that truck could not tree a coon.

After I dropped him off to be with Momma, I decided that I might as well have a cup of coffee before I went back to finish my hunt. I stopped at Carson's Cafe and ordered coffee. As I sipped my coffee, I glanced down at my legs. My blue jeans had turned brown-red and were moving. I was covered with seed ticks.

For those of you who are not personally acquainted with ticks, let me give you a little rundown on them. I will go with the Star Back tick because I find him to be the friendliest of the lot. Momma Star Back fills up with blood from some animal in the spring of the year. This lunch takes about ten days. She mates with Papa Star Back while she fills up with blood. When she gets so full of blood that she is about the size of the first joint in your index finger, she drops off. She climbs a bush or a weed, develops a whole wad of eggs in her distended body, and lays them on the outer extremity of the plant. The eggs hatch into tiny little ticks. They stay in a ball. The first animal that brushes against the plant receives the whole wad of seed ticks. The babies feed, fill up, and drop off. They molt, find another animal, fill up, and drop off again. After several molts we arrive at Momma and Papa Star Back ticks again. If all the baby ticks in all stages were able to find an animal to get on every time they needed one, we would, I am sure, be covered in a six-foot layer of ticks in about two years. I consider what you have just read to be an accurate, short description of a tick cycle, but all my knowledge of them comes from living with them. If some scholar tells you a different story, my advice would be to go with the scholar. I have been known not to have seen what I have seen a number of times in my life.

Anyway I was covered with seed ticks, which was not unusual at all. Sitting there I decided to share my good fortune with my fellow man. I took out my knife and scraped a blade full off my jeans (about a tablespoonful). I carefully raked them off on the stool next to me. I proceeded to leave a wad of ticks on every stool at the counter.

As I drove back out to the Freeman Ranch to continue my hunt, I had a marvelous time trying to imagine how the tourists and truck drivers that frequented Carson's would react to that bunch of biting, itching, festering, worrisome little tick bastards. I felt really good having been able to share my good fortune with someone else.

I have always tried to be generous with ticks. I remember that I went to a wild coon hunt at Bryan, Texas, in probably the spring of 1958. The first person I saw was my old friend Marion Knight. Marion's dog got thrown out of the hunt the first night. I invited him to hunt with me the second night. He replied that he would not go back out in those tick-infested woods for a $1,000 bill.

It became necessary for me to take my truck to haul the hounds in my cast out the second night. I asked Marion if I could leave my bedroll and grub box in his station wagon. He said that would be fine.

Hunt headquarters was in a livestock show barn. We got back in about 2:00 A.M. After we turned in our scorecard, I noticed Marion asleep on a cot in the barn. He was snoring up a storm. He looked lonesome to me. I asked each man in my cast to go to the restroom in the barn and pick his ticks off for me. We put all the ticks in my coffee cup. We ended up with over half a cupful. I took those ticks and dumped them on Marion's pillow. I had picked up a little stick because I thought I would have to herd them, but to my surprise every tick went straight to Marion's bald head. In about twenty minutes Marion came up out of his sack scratching and clawing.

In a little while he told me, "Taylor your sleeping bag must be infested with ticks, and you infested mine when you stored your gear in my station wagon."

I told him that I had slept in my bag that day and I had not noticed any ticks. After a few more minutes of scratching, clawing, and picking, Marion realized that he had been had. This was no accidental infestation. He did his best to find out who was responsible. He never did. I expect he would kill me to this day if he found out I dumped the ticks on him.

Anyway you can see that I am a generous man. Shucks! I am always willing to share a dose of ticks with anybody else.

Funny thing has happened in the last several years. You see, our ding-blasted imported fire ants have all but eliminated ticks in this whole part of the world. Never thought it could happen to me, but you know I sort of miss those friendly little tick bastards.

Big Cat

Bill Kuykendall lived about halfway between Kyle and Driftwood, Texas. I did not know Bill very well, but his brother, Ike, his sister, Dorothy Hoskins, and his sister, Marion Taylor, were close friends of mine. Bill had a pretty good-sized place, and the whole place was fenced with an eight-foot, deer-proof fence. Bill did not allow any trespassing on his place, and at an earlier time before I knew him he killed a young man who was poaching deer on his place. My natural tendency was to give the place a wide berth.

From 1954 until 1964 I did quite a bit of coon hunting around the community of Driftwood. It is a country of caliche hills covered with scrub live oak, cedar, elm, persimmon, algerita, and prickly pear cactus. In those days it was fairly sparsely settled, and it had two good creeks that meandered through it, Gattling Creek and Onion Creek. At that time it supported a healthy coon population. Thanks to people like Clarence Echols, Sid Hall, and Roger Parker, I could hunt almost all the country around Driftwood.

Many of the nights that I hunted in the Driftwood area were weeknights, and I had a store to open the next morning at 7:30. Since a couple of hours of sleep made for an easier day's work, I would usually catch the dogs and head for home at 2 or 3 o'clock in the morning. There were two ways to get from Driftwood to San Marcos, through Kyle and through Wimberly. On those nights I went home through Kyle, I would pass Bill Kuykendall's ranch.

In the spring of 1961, I began to see a bobcat on the road at Bill's place. The cat would hold to my truck's headlights well enough for me to get a good look at him. After I had seen the cat several times, Bill came into the store to buy some livestock product. I told him about seeing the cat. Bill told me he would set traps for him. He had goats, and a bobcat can take a heavy toll on kid goats. Toward the end of summer Bill came in and told me that he had not been able to trap the cat. He said if I ever saw him again to put my hounds on it.

I explained to him that my hounds were broke to run coon only but that I did have two good six-month-old dog pups that I had not started breaking. I also told him because of his reputation concerning trespassers I really chose to stay away from his place. Bill replied that the cat was costing him money and that the hounds and I were more than welcome. My answer was that if I saw that cat I would turn my pups aloose on him. I also promised him that if he made any move to come to me in the pasture he would be in deep trouble. Bill said that was fair enough.

My two pups were Taylor's Blunder and Taylor's Black Bastard. Black and Blunder were litter mates out of my Ruby and McDonalds Nightrider. They were really promising pups, but they were fifteen or twenty pounds larger than I wanted a coonhound. They were good strike dogs, excellent trail hounds, and fair on the tree. By one of those quirks of luck, both dogs were physically destroyed on a hunt in 1963. The hunt was on Sally Faber's place off the Devilsbackbone in what is now part of Canyon Lake. Black got his head bashed in from a fall off a bluff and Blunder had both front feet ruined at a hole in which he ran a coon. He stayed at the hole he ran the coon in. I could not get to him or call him off for two nights and a day. When he finally left the hole, the coon had chewed the toes off both front feet. He never recovered enough to be able to run, and I finally destroyed him.

One night after fall rolled around as I started home from Driftwood, I spotted the bobcat on the road. He went through the fence into the Kuykendall place. I unloaded Black and Blunder, who were then nine- or ten-months old. As soon as they smelled the cat, they opened on the tracks. They trailed up to the fence. I kicked the bottom staples out at a post, lifted up the fence, and they went under and away on the fresh cat tracks. Those pups were driving that cat like old seasoned hounds. They had only gone three- or four-hundred yards when they began to tree. I walked up to about twenty yards of the tree, a mesquite, and turned on my light and looked for the cat. When the beam from my light hit him, he jumped from the tree and the race was on again. Within a quarter of a mile the cat had gotten into some thick cactus, catclaw, and algerita. The race slowed down and the cat would duck and dodge, creep and sneak. After some minutes of this, Black got up on him and made him run. He left out toward a little creek with a bluff on the north side of it, but before he got there the dogs forced him up another mesquite tree.

I hunted with a big six-cell flashlight with a rheostat switch. I had a fine Smith & Wesson K-22 pistol on my belt. As I approached this second tree, I stopped when I was about fifty yards from it. I barely turned the flashlight on and swung the beam past the mesquite tree. While the dim light did not reveal any details, I was able to pick up the cat's eyes. I got my pistol out of its holster and cocked it in preparation for a shot. I roughly lined up the pistol sights, and with my left hand I started turning up the rheostat switch. The cat held the tree. When the light was at full capacity, I was able to see the cat almost as well as I could have in daylight. My sights were lined up on his shoulder. I increased pressure on the trigger. When the trigger broke, I knew it was a good shot. The cat fell almost at the sound of the shot. I hurried to the tree and took the cat away from Black and Blunder.

When I got back to the truck, I looked the cat over. He looked big, but he felt light. I have a picture of the bobcat, Black, Blunder, my little gray Ford truck, and me. As I hold the cat by the hind legs, with my hand shoulder high, his front legs almost touch the ground. That would make him stretch out to about four feet long. When I got to town, I stopped by the store and weighed him. He weighed exactly 8¾ pounds. An average mature house cat will weigh ten pounds. I left him at the store.

The next morning I asked quite a number of knowledgeable outdoor farm and ranch people to tell me how much he weighed. Jack Olden from Wimberly thought twenty-two pounds. Ben Simon from Wimberly said maybe twenty pounds. Friday Ellis from San Marcos thought twenty pounds. Dare Williams from San Marcos indicated eighteen pounds. Travis Tate from Hunter was sure he would weigh twenty pounds. The heaviest guess was twenty-two pounds, the smallest eighteen. That cat had the frame and fur of a large bobcat. He was just unusually lean. I do not have an explanation for it.

We hunters do have a tendency to overestimate the weight of animals we kill or catch. As a matter of fact, accurate scales would take half the fun out of hunting and fishing. I have seen quite a number of 100- to 110-pound deer shrink to 65 pounds when exposed to a set of accurate scales. I have seen even more 20- and 25-pound coons come down to 12 pounds when weighed. If you ever want to ruin a good fish story, just throw a set of scales at that 6½-pound bass or 25-pound yellow catfish.

H. A. Wallace

It has been a long time since I have seen Red Wallace. Changes of jobs and changes in where we lived separated us. I could not for certain tell you where I first met H. A. Wallace but I would bet it was at some wild coon hunt in the early 1950s. He lived in San Antonio. I lived in San Marcos. I do remember the first time he came to San Marcos to hunt with me. I took him to some country between Staples and Kingsbury. That country and the coons could certainly test a hound's pedigree. That country and those coons would also test a hunter's resolve.

Gus Eoff went with us that night. Red brought a little white Walker hound with a tan head named White Man and a medium-sized bluetick whose name I do not remember. Gus turned aloose Ol' Shotsie and Ginger. I hunted Ruby and Rastus. It was interesting to me that our hounds would not honor each other. For the first several coons, Gus's dogs and my dogs worked together while Red's hounds worked to themselves on another coon. I could tell from the first coon that White Man was a good hound. After the separate packs had treed and killed a couple of coons, they started honoring each other and working together. As soon as our combined hounds started working a coon, I could tell that White Man was one fine coonhound. We hunted long and hard that night, and by the end of the night I was convinced that Red and his hounds were the kind you like to hunt with.

I had better hunting country and much more of it than Red did; consequently, he came to hunt with me most of the time. We did not hunt together with any frequency, probably averaging a couple of hunts a year for eight or nine years. Our wives got to know each other, and, on a number of hunts, Red would bring Madeline. Billye and Madeline would visit while we hunted. Those two women were world-class coffee drinkers and would consume pot after pot of coffee until we came in from hunting.

As I said, Red was the kind of hunter you liked to hunt with. His hounds were above average, and you could depend on them being solid broke. When things went wrong, I never remember Red complaining, and, to show a most remarkable facet of his personality, I never remember hearing him brag on his dogs either. Even more remarkable, I do not remember ever hearing him make excuses for his hounds. If he used alcohol in any fashion, it was certainly not while hunting, and I do not remember that he used tobacco either. His mouth was clean and his word was good. He was a good hound man. He is a good man.

I bred my Taylor's Black Ruby to Burn's Black Rocket. Four days after she whelped, Ruby died. Billye helped me try to save the surviving pups, three little bitches. First we lost one to hookworms and the effects of the then-new shot for hookworms. Then I was able to locate a cur-bitch with a fresh litter. I put the two remaining pups on this bitch. The cur-bitch bit one of these pups in the head and damaged its brain, leaving me with one pup. This pup survived, and I named her Taylor's Black Ruby II. I started taking her to the woods before she was two months old. I can remember finishing a number of hunts with Ruby in my jumper pocket after she had worn herself out trying to keep up with me.

When my pup was about three months old, I got a phone call from Red. He told me he had heard that I had lost Ol' Ruby. He expressed his concern over my loss. He was happy to hear that I was able to save one of the pups. He asked if I had anything to work the pup with. I told him I would have to hunt her with Gus and his hounds.

Red then made me a most remarkable offer. He stated that his dad, who lived at Hearn, had, in order to collect a debt, been forced to take a coonhound in on part of the debt. Red stated that he now had this hound and that he found him to absolutely not run any trash. He told me I could take this hound, use him for as long as it took me to train my pup, and then return him. I asked what my responsibilities were if something happened to the dog. He replied that I would owe him nothing as he knew I would treat the dog as if it were mine. I asked when I could get this hound, and he suggested that I pick it up Sunday afternoon.

Sunday, I loaded Billye and the kids in my little red Ford pickup and headed to San Antonio. Billye and the kids stayed to visit with Madeline and her kids while Red and I went to his dog pens that were several miles from his house. On the way to the pens, Red told me not to let this dog's looks fool me as he was a really fine hound. Even with this warning I was not prepared for what I saw. He looked like a cross between a hound and a German shepherd. He was black and tan with his black being mostly a black saddle. His ears turned down, but they did not turn very far down. I exclaimed that he was just a big cur-dog. Red assured me that he was a fine hound with a good nose and that he would absolutely not run trash. I took the dog home.

Monday night I went hunting with Red's dog and my pup. Red's dog followed never more than a step behind me all night. Wednesday night I hunted again with the same result. Saturday night I took him with Gus's dogs. Gus's bitches did their usual excellent work and showed us a number of coons. Red's dog held his usual position, about one step behind me, during the running, during the treeing, and during the fighting of the coon.

I called Red Sunday and told him that maybe I should return his dog as he would not hit a lick for me. Red explained that that was the way he had been when he first got him, but after a while he got over it. He suggested I just keep on working him. Since I had every confidence in Red and his knowledge of hounds, I set out to get his dog accustomed to me. I hunted him night after night, sometimes alone, sometimes with Gus's dogs. Most times with Gus's dogs I would tie them off when they treed, and jump the treed coon out on Red's dog. He would just stand there and watch the coon run off. As Red said, he sure did not run any trash.

He did not run any trash that is until one night he stumbled up on an armadillo. When the armadillo broke and ran, that dog took in after him and ran him to his hole. He even barked at the hole a couple of times. A few nights later he silently chased a jack rabbit a little way, but he was soon back to his usual position of right behind me. A few nights later he spotted a deer at one of Eb Horner's wild turkey feeders. He took in after the deer and ran him out of the range of my flashlight, but he was soon back to his usual position, right behind me.

That night he also ran a coon we jumped out on him, but he only ran it for as long as he could see it. He would not work an animal by scent, only by sight.

I told Gus I was sure a slow learner and awful dumb, but that I finally realized that serious, firm, solid Ol' Red had pulled a fast one on me. That blamed dog was just a cur-dog Red had picked up off the streets of San Antonio to play a joke on me. It had never been in the woods before I took it. I had a single-shot .22 rifle under the seat of my truck. I killed the cur dog. Then I started racking my brain because in some way I had to get even with Red.

I called Red that night and told him that his Ol' dog had finally started working a little for me. That he was treeing pretty good with Gus's dogs and that he was a coon-killing machine. Red had told me his dad had not told him what the dog's name was, so I told Red I had named him Pecker. Weeks later I called Red and told him that Ol' Pecker was really eating a tree up and that he would simply inhale a coon when it was shook out on him. I also told him that Pecker was running a little with Gus's dogs.

I waited a few weeks and called Red again. I bragged on what a fine tree dog and kill dog Pecker was. I also said that Pecker was running pretty good and even hunting a little. I told him my little Ruby pup was working pretty well with him. I then sat back and waited to let the wheels turn in Red's head.

Some weeks passed before Red called me to ask how his dog was doing. I told him that he had really come to himself and was finding, running, treeing, and killing coons all by himself. I explained that my Ruby pup was hunting pretty well, running pretty well, and treeing pretty well, all thanks to Ol' Pecker.

The next day after work I drove all over San Marcos. I finally spotted a cur dog that looked almost exactly like the dog I got from Red. He was at José Alvarado's house. José was a friend of mine. I asked him whose dog it was. José told me it was just a dog that hung around and was a nuisance to everyone. I told José if he would help me catch him I would haul him off. José gave me a hand.

That blamed dog got car sick in the dog box on my truck on the way home. I had to haul him in my dog box for three days before he got over it. Then I called Red and told him my Ruby pup was working real well and that I planned to work her by herself for a few months to keep her from being dependent on another dog's work. Red suggested that he come hunting Saturday night and pick up his dog then. I sure had to figure out a way to keep from going to the woods with the new Pecker and Red. I invented plans that Billye and I had for Saturday night. I told Red that fortunately I had a business meeting in San Antonio on Friday night and that I would deliver the dog on the way to the meeting. I delivered the dog that Friday evening after work. I thanked Red for the use of his dog. I bragged on what a fine coon dog he was once he got used to me.

You know, I didn't hear from Ol' Red for ever so long a time. Months and months and months later I ran into him at a wild coon hunt close to Elgin. I immediately asked Red how Ol' Pecker was doing. Red said it was a sad story but Ol' Pecker had died on a coon hunt. Said he just fell over dead.

Later I visited with one of his hunting buddies. He stated that Red worked with that cur-dog almost two months trying to get it to do what I said it would do. He related that he was with Red the night he realized he had been had. He said Red got a single-shot .22 out from under the seat of his truck and dispatched Ol' Pecker. He stated that Red repeated over and over on the way home that he could not understand how he could have been so dumb as to fall for my story.

As I stated earlier, I haven't seen or heard from Red in a long time, maybe twenty-five years. But you can believe we share a kinship that neither time nor distance will diminish. It has been the special relationship with hunters such as Clarence Echols, Gus Eoff, C. C. Hancock, and Red Wallace that has helped make being a hound man the fine experience it has been for me. Great hunters are like great hounds. There are not many of them out there, but a good hound or a good hunter is a pure delight when you do find one. Red Wallace and his White Man were both a pure delight.

C. C. Hancock

I was camped at the Texas State Championship Wild Coon Hunt at Mexia. I had brought my little Black and Tan bitch, Taylor's Black Ruby II, to hunt. She was probably two years old at the time. I came a day early just for the pleasure of visiting and hunting with other early arrivers. I stirred up my fire and put on a pot of coffee. About the time I poured the first cup, a man walked into my camp. I offered coffee. He accepted. His name was C. C. Hancock. I had met him there at the hunt several years before. He lived in Carnegie, Oklahoma. We arranged to hunt together that night.

We had a good hunt, and we treed a number of coons. This hunt left no doubt in my mind that Mr. Hancock was hunting a fine blue hound and that Mr. Hancock knew hounds as well as any man I had ever been to the woods with. Through our conversations during this hunt, I learned that Mr. Hancock owned a general store that his wife mostly ran, that he hauled and sold minnows for fish bait, and that he would offer to buy a good hound when he saw one.

The luck of the draw threw us together in the same cast the first night of the hunt. The other two dogs in our cast were not in the same class as his blue dog and my Ruby bitch, and our two hounds scored a bunch of plus points, while the other two dogs went in the hole. About midnight the dogs struck a cold track, so everyone, judge, guide, and handlers sat down to rest while the hounds worked the track out. After a while they jumped the coon, and the race was on. We started the process of following the dogs. I was slow to get up, and everyone had walked off by the time I was on my feet. When I switched on my light, I spotted a billfold lying on the ground. That was the fattest billfold I have ever seen. I called to the departing hunters and asked who had lost a billfold. Hancock came back and claimed it.

He opened up the billfold and offered me a hundred-dollar bill. I told him I did not want his money. He showed me the money. It looked to be all hundred-dollar bills. To me it looked to be many more than fifty of them. As I said, when Hancock saw a good coonhound he tried to buy it, cash money on the line. For the rest of that hunt every time I turned around Hancock was trying to buy me something to eat.

The next year, as usual, I was camped at Mexia a day early in order to enjoy some visiting and hunting before the actual hunt began. Hancock showed up with three or four Oklahoma hunters. He suggested he and I make a hunt that night. We cast our hounds about 9:00 P.M. and had some dandy races. In a conversation on the way in I mentioned that my Ruby bitch would tree coons in the daytime at almost the same rate she treed them at night.

We got back to camp about 5:00 A.M. I tied Ol' Ruby to a fence post and rolled up in a G. I. blanket in the back of my truck for some sleep. About thirty minutes later, at daylight, one of the Oklahoma hunters shook my shoulder. At that stage of my life, thanks to the U.S. Government, I did not do gentle wake-ups. Before I knew what was happening I had reached up, grabbed that ol' boy by the guzzle and pulled him half over the side of my truck. About that time, I realized where I was and what was happening, so no real harm was done. I got up, put on coffee, and asked what he wanted. He said that Hancock had told him that I had said that Ruby would tree coons in the daytime. He said he found that hard to believe and that he would like to see it done. We drank some coffee, and I pitched Ol' Ruby into the back of the truck. I told him to get in the truck because we were going to see how a good hound can tree coons in the daytime—whether he was ready or not.

We went to the post oak country close to Groesbeck. As we started our hunt, I took my little chopping ax from the truck. Ol' Ruby struck a fresh track soon after I cast her. After a hot, fast race of only a few minutes, she nailed the tree. When we got to the tree, we found it to be a large hollow post oak. The coon was not on the outside. I made the statement that as far as I was concerned that was one coon treed and that if he had any doubts I had the ax for him to cut to the hollow in order to see the coon. He told me he was satisfied there was a coon there.

I led Ruby away from the tree and cast her again. She struck after a while a good way from us. It was a good-moving track, and in less than a half-hour she barked up. When we got to her, we found her treed on an elm tree beside a little creek. The coon was medium sized and was on the outside right at the top of the tree.

During the next couple of hours we treed two more coons, one outside and one inside a hollow. Starvation was beginning to plague my stomach, so I asked the Oklahoma fellow if he was convinced Ol' Ruby could tree coons in the daytime. He indicated he was satisfied. In fact, he said he thought she had done a fine job of it.

After we got back to camp, I tied Ruby to a fence post and built up my fire. I made coffee and fried some sausage. I ended the meal with some of Billye's good oatmeal cookies and coffee. Ol' Ruby always was a nervous dog and the strange campgrounds and the park full of hounds caused her to whine and bark excessively. I scolded her as I started to lie down in the back of my truck for some much needed sleep and rest.

Before I could close my eyes another of the Oklahoma hunters walked up and asked if Ruby was always that noisy. I told him not really. He asked if she was that mouthy in the woods. Was she a babbler? I lost my temper. I told him he could get his butt in my little Ford pickup and find out if she babbled or I was going to kick his butt.

We went to some country east of Groesbeck on the Navasota River. It was pretty thick brush, but nothing had any thorns. Ruby did some fine work and treed a number of daytime coons. As usual she used her mouth perfectly on trail and on tree. Late in the afternoon I asked the ol' boy if he had seen enough. He said he sure had. I asked if Ruby babbled. He replied, "No, sir."

We were back in camp before dark. I tied Ruby to a fence post and built up my fire. Before I could cook anything to eat Marion Knight invited me to share a pot of stew he had just finished cooking. It was good stew. About the time we finished eating, they started the drawing of the packs for the first night's hunt. So, it was load up the hounds and back to the woods for the night's hunt. About 3:00 A.M. my cast had finished and we stopped at an all-night cafe in Groesbeck for coffee. By 4:00 A.M. we were back in camp. I was too sleepy and tired to cook anything. I just fed Ruby, tied her to a fence post, and rolled up in my G. I. blanket in back of my truck.

Before good daylight someone slapped the side of my truck. As I said earlier, I did not do gentle wake-ups then. I was on my feet and out of my truck with my chopping ax in my hands before I knew where I was and what was going on. The third Oklahoma hunter was backing up and looking at me a little wild eyed. I asked what he wanted. He said that his hunting buddies were talking about Ruby's ability to tree coons in the daytime and that he sure would like to see it done. I replied that I had not had any real sleep in at least the past forty-eight hours. He replied that if I was not tough enough, then he expected that he could live without seeing if Ruby could tree daytime coons. I answered that since I was awake and since I had come to hunt, we might as well go. I also told him that if there were any more Oklahoma sons-of-bitches who wanted to see Ruby work in the daytime, then he had best get them all gathered up for this hunt.

At about noon we were back in camp. Ruby had done some fine work. Most of the coons she treed had been on the outside. I built up my fire, made coffee, and fried potatoes and eggs. As I finished, Hancock walked into camp. He accepted a cup of coffee. As he drank the coffee, he asked if I would like to make a short hunt before the drawing for the casts of that night's hunt.

It hit me like a bolt of lightning. Hancock, with the help of his Oklahoma friends, was checking out the pedigree of both Ruby and me. For whatever reason he was trying to run Ol' Ruby and me both out. I told him I thought an afternoon hunt was a good idea. We got back to camp just in time for the drawings. Ruby looked pretty good. I was plumb fizzle-sprung after more than sixty hours with little or no sleep or rest.

My cast made a pretty good hunt of it that night. Ruby did all I could have expected of her with mostly first strikes and first trees. I, probably because of fatigue, made several bad calls on her that cost a bunch of points. We did not place in the top-ten dogs in the hunt, but I was proud of the way she had stood up to the abuse I had allowed to be heaped on her.

During the drive home, I gave a lot of thought as to why Hancock and his Oklahoma hunters had set out to wear us down. My conclusion was that Hancock either wanted to see how dumb I really was or that it was his idea of a big joke.

The next year I did not make the hunt at Mexia because Ruby had pups. Then we missed the following year because Ruby had a terrible injury. The year after that Ruby and I did make it back to the Texas State Hunt, but I had just gotten out of the hospital after a painful operation, and I really was in no condition to be in the woods. Then I got caught in a job change and missed making the hunt for four more years. Ol' Ruby must have been about eleven years old before I felt even in a position where I could run her at Mexia, but by then she was old and worn-out. I could not do anything about the old and worn-out, but the year she was twelve, I had her in the best condition it was possible for her to be in.

I went to Mexia early. You know, to visit and hunt. Hancock walked into my camp shortly after I got there. He looked at Ruby and stated that I surely did not plan to enter her. I answered that was what I came for. He replied he did not think she could finish the hunt. I told him to just hide and watch us.

Ol' Ruby was just a shadow of her former self. She had lost her blazing speed. She no longer searched for coons in a manner that would make one think she had them locked in on radar. But you know that ol' bitch fooled me. That first night she got more than her share of first strikes. She was right up in the front of the pack the whole night. She never made a mistake on a tree, and we got a good portion of the first trees. Son! She done good.

It was about an hour-and-a-half ride back from where my cast hunted to camp. By the time we got there, Ruby was so knocked out and stove up from her tremendous effort, that she would not unload. I pulled her out of the truck and offered her feed. She would not eat. I looked over her feet and legs and removed all the thorns I could find. That was about all I could do for her. I tied her to a fence post, crawled up in the back of my truck, and went to sleep.

I woke up with a start because I heard Ruby whimper. I sat up and looked at her. There was Hancock. He was rubbing her legs down with liniment. After he had rubbed each leg, shoulder, and hip down, he turned her over and treated the bottoms of her feet with Pad Kote, a product made to help tender, damaged feet. Then he went back to his truck and got what looked to me like cooked beef steak. He cut it up in small pieces and got her to eat it. I lay back down, and he never knew I saw him.

I spent a good deal of time thinking about why Hancock was trying to get Ruby in shape to run the second night. I finally decided that in her prime he would have gone to almost any length to beat her, but that as an ol' worn-out bitch he respected and loved her just as I did for what she had once been. Now that is a sportsman.

Ol' Ruby fired up the next night, but she just could not compete. We had to settle for third and fourth strikes and third and fourth trees, but we did finish the hunt. We never scored a minus point the whole hunt.

The next morning before I left for home, Hancock came by and took me to breakfast. We had a good visit, but, you know, he never mentioned anything about helping Ol' Ruby so she could finish the hunt. He simply said he thought she had done well considering her age and the dumb handler she had. We parted, and I have not seen or heard from Hancock since then.

In the time I knew Hancock, we probably never spent, all put together, as much as a week with each other. But I think I know the man.

During the twenty years since I have seen Hancock, a number of hunters have come to me asking where they could buy a top coonhound. I always answer C. C. Hancock, Carnegie, Oklahoma. I tell them any hound he offers for sale is as good as he says it is because his word is good. Then I caution them that if they go to a hunt with him to be careful. When it is his time to climb the tree and shake out the coon, they should run backward. You see, Mr. Hancock will probably reach in his pocket, take out his false teeth, and hand them over to be held. He will say he does not want to risk breaking them if he falls out of the tree.

Hit 'Em Out Old Lady

My oldest son, Tom, asked me to take him hunting one Saturday afternoon in the fall of 1969. Said he would like for me to just take Ol' Ruby, as he knew that since she was thirteen she could not hunt much longer.

Before anyone snorts too loudly about coon hunting in the daytime, just let me state that for her lifetime Ruby was able to tree coons in the daytime at only a slightly slower pace than at night. The year she was four years old she averaged treeing a coon about every twenty minutes at night and one every thirty minutes during the day. The main difference between the two was that the daytime coons would be in a hollow 50 percent of the time. Hunters even came from other states to see her do this, and she never failed to show them daytime coons.

Tom and I went to Ed Posey's place. We cast her in his east pasture. She left hunting in a long swinging trot, and I heard her strike before Tom and I had gone a hundred yards. At this stage of her life, she had lost a great deal of her once spectacular speed on a hot track; consequently, her races were longer because she would not push the coon hard enough to make him go up. During her later years, watching her work a coon track was watching a true work of art. For a real hound man, it was a thing of beauty, no wasted motion, all done in a smooth flow and punctuated with chop and bawl mouth used to perfection. When the coon went up, she would run up the tree giving trail mouth for six or eight feet. Then as she fell back toward the ground, she would change to a tree mouth with a big joyful squall and start treeing with a ringing chop when she hit the ground. Hot damn, but it makes the hair stand up on the back of my neck just to think about it.

That coon went into the King place, and Ruby nailed him to the tree. The tree had a hollow, but the coon was on the outside. I handed my pistol to Tom and told him to bring the coon out, but to make sure he was dead as I did not want Ruby to have to fight him. Tom made a good shot, and Ruby really enjoyed mauling the dead coon.

I hung the coon up in a fork of the tree and led Ruby away. After a couple of hundred yards I cast her again. She left going south. We went to the top of a good hill and stopped and listened, but she had not struck. Finally we walked on south to another hill, but we did not hear anything there either. After a couple of hours I became a little concerned. I had noticed in the several months preceding this hunt that Ruby had lost the ability to home back in after a hunt. I would have to find her and lead her in. Tom and I walked back to the truck and drove around to the King place. From the highest hill in that part of the country we could not hear her. About dark we went home.

I got my light, my coffee pot, and my blowing horn. I drove all over that country. I did not hear her. Finally I went back to the high hill in the King place and put on the coffee pot. I stayed the night, but I heard nothing. I blew my horn every once in a while, but she did not come in. After daylight I drove to all the houses in that part of the world, from Tom Brown Martin's to Charles Rector Williams's. No one had seen or heard her.

I went home, had breakfast, and slept until noon. That Sunday afternoon I again covered the country, listening and looking for her with no success. That night I covered adjoining country to the north, the west, and the south. I called with my blowing horn and listened. Still I could find no sign of her.

There was no doubt in my mind that if she came into any of the ranch houses in that part of the world the people at the ranch would have called me. All of those people knew her. Most had hunted with her.

Monday morning I called my office at College Station and changed my itinerary so that I could come home each night and continue to look for her. During the nights that week, I went to almost every dirt stock tank in the area looking for her tracks. I could find no sign of her.

I had a young bitch at that time that was a fair hound. She was broke and she could tree most of her coons. Hoping that Ruby would hear and come in, I ran her every night that week. Still no success. When Sunday night came around, I was tired and sleepy and discouraged. There was no way that I could continue to believe that Ruby was still alive. I stayed home and rested.

The next week my responsibilities at work were so pressing that it was necessary for me to be gone for the whole week. That weekend I again covered the country listening, calling with my horn, and looking for signs of her.

As the next week started, I had an obligation to be in Kerrville for a court case I had filed there. The case was not finished until late Tuesday afternoon. I decided to spend the night at Kerrville. I checked into a motel, and after watching the news I went to eat. When I arrived back at my room an hour or so later, the phone was ringing. It was Billye.

A bus driver for the New Braunfels school district had picked Ruby up off the road that afternoon between Hunter and New Braunfels. He called Billye and chewed her out for letting a dog get in the shape Ruby was in. Billye found out where he lived, and she and Tom went after her. After Billye explained the circumstances, the bus driver apologized for his harsh words. They took Ruby home and called me.

I loaded up and headed home. Never in my life have I seen a hound in such a condition. Looking at her, it was hard to believe that she was still living. Her normal weight was 45 pounds. On my bathroom scales as I held her in my arms, we weighed 177 pounds. That meant she only weighed 17 pounds. All the meat on her muzzle was worn away from trailing. There were no lips in front, just bare teeth. The bottoms of her feet were nothing but raw meat and bones. Most of her toenails were gone. The front of her hind legs and the fronts of her shoulders were slipping hair and hide from a mass of cactus thorns in them. The tip of her tail was bare bone. Her ears were swollen and torn in a number of places. Her eyes were matted up. Her body was nothing but a skeleton covered with hide.

Billye had fed her a little roast gravy over dry dog food. The next morning I got her to eat a pretty good bit of cornbread, boiled liver, and the juice from the boiled liver. From that point on she started mending. In a couple of weeks her lips were mostly grown back, but it was months before they changed from pink to her normal black. After a month she looked pretty good. Just awfully thin. By spring she looked fine.

I do not know what happened to Ruby during the seventeen days she was lost. My best educated guess is that she trailed and treed coons the whole time. Old age had taken her ability to keep from getting lost. Under that handicap I think she did the only other thing she knew to do. Start, trail, and tree coons. Her gameness had already been demonstrated to the world. I do not think she ever actually quit in that seventeen days. She may have slept, but she never quit.

For the whole of Ruby's adult life she was a fool over Billye's cornbread. For the remainder of her life, Billye gave her a fresh pan of cornbread every once in a while. She also was fond of a little coffee over some sugar. I am pretty sure Billye saw that she got that every once in a while too. I never took her hunting again.

As the summer of 1970 passed, Ruby became progressively more feeble. I noticed that in August she was drinking large quantities of water. One evening late in August, Billye and I started to take her for a walk. She was so feeble she could hardly walk. Her kidneys were almost shut down. She was in tough shape. I knew the end was near. My first reaction was to take her the next day to a veterinarian and let him kill her for me. She hated a veterinarian office so badly that I ruled out that idea.

I went to the house and got my shotgun, some shells, and my light. I picked up Ruby and set her in the truck seat. I drove her to the caliche pit on Preston King's place. We had hunted from that pit many times. I took her in my arms and set her down on the ground. I told her, "Let's go Ol' Lady, hit 'em out." She looked at me and switched her tail. Then she started shuffling to the woods. I let her get to the edge of the brush, and I took her down with a 20-gauge load to the back of the head at point-blank range. It was instant death. I put the gun in the truck. I took her collar off and put it in the truck.

I sat down and cried for a while. I thought about the almost fourteen years that we had shared with each other. I realized just how much I had loved that old bitch. I also realized how much I was going to miss her. I cried a little more and then went home.

Without my having told her, Billye knew what I had done. When I got home we spent some time sharing with each other our feelings. I told Billye that I was through coon hunting. I had hunted with what I considered the very best. I had no interest in a futile search for Ruby's replacement.

I had a fair young coonhound bitch in my pen. I gave her away. In the twenty-five years since Ruby's death I have not been back to the woods coon hunting. I have never had a desire to go.

Clarence and Edith Echols

I was hunting animal-feed customers, and I was beating the bushes for them in the Texas Hill Country northwest of San Marcos. The year was 1954, and the bulk of the animals I was trying to sell feed for were range cattle, sheep, and Angora goats. I was working against a stacked deck. First we were in the middle of a horrible drought and many of the range animals in the hill country had been sold because of this drought. My second problem was that because of the extended effects of this drought, few of the Hill Country ranchers had money to pay for feed for their animals. My third problem was that my prospective customers were already buying all the feed they could afford from more local businesses that were run by their friends and neighbors. I had been at this chore, full-time, for over a month. Constant rejections had me feeling dejected, disheartened, and slap-dab discouraged.

I followed a dusty, rocky, caliche ranch road, off a dusty, rocky, caliche county road that ran west from Driftwood. The ranch road went through typical Hill Country land that even under the best of conditions supported far too many rocks and far too little grass. There was an abundance of scrub live oak, algerita, cedar, black persimmon, along with a sprinkling of prickly pear cactus. I came to a typical Hill Country house of that time, weather beaten, front porch that ran the length of the house, an add-on room or two to accommodate the second generation, with a corrugated tin roof. People who depended on this stingy land for a living could little afford the luxury of paint for the house.

It was midafternoon and there was not much spring to my gait as I stepped up on the porch. I was hot, tired, sweaty, and discouraged. Before I could knock on the door, a lady stepped to the door and asked if she could help me. I introduced myself and told her I would sure like to talk to her husband. She said, "That's too bad because Clarence, my husband, is off helping a neighbor work sheep." I started to leave, and as I was stepping off the porch the lady told me she had just finished baking a batch of cookies. She asked if I would like some coffee and cookies before I left.

My natural inclination was to say thanks but no thanks. This was a lone woman in an isolated place. I really felt like giving the lady a lecture about offering strangers access to her home, but there was something about the lady that made me feel completely at ease, and she certainly was at ease with me. So I replied that the coffee sure sounded good. I also said since it was so hot I would like the coffee out on the porch. She came out in a short time with a glass percolator coffee pot full of fresh hot coffee, cups, and a plate of cookies. Good coffee? Coffee does not get any better than that coffee. Good cookies? They were about as good as Billye's. She told me her name was Edith, Edith Echols. We talked. We talked weather. We talked dry. We talked dust. We talked children. She had two boys, Tommy and Shelby. I spotted a pen off northeast of the house. I said it looked like a dog pen. She said Clarence had a pack of foxhounds. My! My!

About the time I finished my second cup of coffee and the biggest part of the plate of cookies, I heard a truck rattling along the rocky caliche road. Edith told me that that would be her husband, Clarence.

Clarence was a pretty good-sized man. He had a hawk beak nose, eyes that squinted from too much exposure to a glaring sun, legs that were about half a foot too long for his body, huge hands, early worry lines from too much stress from drought conditions, and a beat-up old hat that I thought might have been a hand-me-down from his daddy.

I liked Edith before I tasted her coffee. I liked Clarence before I shook his hand. After I introduced myself, Clarence had a cup of coffee. I started the conversation with hounds. Ol' Clarence talked hound pretty well. I drifted the conversation to range cubes for cattle and sheep and corn for the goats. Clarence said he would have to think about that for a while. I figured I had about used up my welcome, so I thanked them and left.

Well, I let Ol' Clarence think about buying feed from me for about a week, and then I went back by to ask for his business again.

Found Clarence at home this time. Got some more good coffee along with the best dried sausage I have ever eaten. The thought of that coffee, dried sausage, and soda crackers, even though it was forty years ago, makes me slobber today. When one has eaten some of Clarence Echols' dried sausage, then all other sausage is only a poor imitation. The raising of the hogs, butchering of the hogs, hunting of the deer, processing of the deer, grinding of the meat, mixing meat and seasoning, stuffing the casings, smoking and drying the meat, all add up to a major expenditure of time and effort. Many people paint; few produce art. Many people write; few produce literature. Many people make sausage; there is only one Clarence Echols.

After my fourth or fifth trip by to visit with Clarence about buying feed, he gave me an order for some range cubes and corn. In a reasonably short time, Clarence had not only developed into a fine customer, he was helping me sell feed to his neighbors.

We saw each other at least once a week. We visited about weather, cows, sheep, goats, and prices. Every time we got together, we talked hounds too. One day Clarence asked me if my hounds were broke. Boy! Did I jump on that, "Solid broke as a rock. Nothing but coon!" Clarence suggested I bring the hounds up hunting the next night.

I took Shotsie and Ruby up to the Echols place. We cast from the house. We had gotten no farther than a hundred yards before Shotsie ran across a possum. She did not open on the possum but grabbed it and shook it. You could always depend on Clarence to be looking where he had no business looking.

Before Shotsie could turn the possum aloose and go on hunting, I heard Clarence say, "You said solid broke. Nothing but coon."

I tried to defend Ol' Shotsie. I claimed she had not opened on or run the possum. She merely pinched it. Clarence replied that any dog that caught a possum was not a broke dog. I will not stretch this night any longer, mainly because the dogs did not work well that night. Anyway Clarence invited me back for another hunt, and over a period of time I got to where I hunted at Driftwood pretty regularly—mostly because I found Clarence to be one of the most knowledgeable hound men I have ever hunted with. A second reason was I liked to hunt with him. The only bad habit I ever knew Clarence to have was chewing tobacco. If he ever drank alcohol, I sure never knew about it. His mouth was clean. His word was good. And finally the people in the community all held him in high regard. Clarence was and is a true gentleman and a true sportsman.

There was one thing I had to get used to with Clarence. I was accustomed to joshing, teasing, and prank playing while out hunting with my friends. I also used my sharp quick tongue to good advantage. With Clarence I never had a chance. He would get me on the defensive, and when I flinched he would jump in for the kill. He could sure lay his tongue on me and my dogs.

I have some rules: I do not loan my chopping ax. I do not loan my guns. I do not loan my truck, and I sure do not loan out my dogs. However, if Clarence ever wanted to borrow any of these things from me, he could have them in a heartbeat. In 1966 Billye and I moved down from Amarillo to Beeville. I started down to Beeville to make arrangements for a house for us to live in. I took Ruby with me and asked Clarence to keep her for me till I came for her. I think I told him to hunt her like she was his. I probably left her there for a couple of months. There was not another person in this world I would have left her with.

The only weak spot I ever found in Clarence was his sincere belief that he could shoot a pistol. The fact of the matter is Clarence was only a fair-to-middling pistol shot. Let me give you an example. I once told Clarence I was going to hunt the Cox ranch, which as I remember was about eight miles from Driftwood. Clarence said he sure would like to hunt there with me. If I remember, he wanted the coons for their hides. We went on a Saturday night, and it seems to me that his two boys, Shelby and Tommy, went with us. Shelby was carrying a High Standard .22 revolver, and I carried a Smith & Wesson K-22. As we treed coons, we took turns shooting them out. When it came time for Clarence to shoot, the dogs had a big coon up a medium-sized live oak tree. Let me emphasize, I mean big as in humongous. I looked at that coon and told Clarence that I did not want Ruby to have to fight that big thing. I told him to shoot the coon through the head so he would come out dead. Clarence told me he would to better than that; he would shoot the coon through the eye. He informed me that any average pistol shooter could hit a coon in the head, but only an expert (like him) could shoot the coon through the eye.

Shelby gave him his pistol. I held my big six-cell light on the coon that was not more than fifteen feet away. Clarence yanked off his shot. At the shot that big sucker came tumbling out of the tree.

Ol' Clarence said, "Well boys! That's the way it's supposed to be done. He is dead as a doornail."

When the coon hit the ground, the dogs grabbed him. That dead coon came alive and whipped the ding-dong-diddle-dee out of my dogs. Seems I can remember having to pitch in and help the poor ol' dogs. I also seem to remember he chewed a little of the diddle-dee out of me too.

When the old boar was finally dead, I picked him up and told Clarence to show me his "eye" shot. Clarence shone his light on the coon and after a long search he pointed to the coon's right eye. The eye was a little damaged, but I maintained one of the dogs bit him there. Clarence argued that any idiot could see and recognize the work of an expert eye-shooter. Anyway, we never settled the argument, but I still maintain that Clarence cannot shoot a pistol from shucks.

When we finished the hunt, Clarence and his boys loaded the coons and left for Driftwood. I left for home. Tommy told me later that Clarence had weighed that big boar coon on a cotton balance beam scale. If I remember correctly, he said it weighed 17¾ pounds. In my lifetime I have killed only one other coon that weighed that much. It was an old three-legged boar. All the rest of the thousands of coons I have killed weighed at least 2¾ less than that.

Billye and I went to Driftwood a couple of years ago to celebrate Clarence and Edith's fiftieth wedding anniversary. The event was held in the Driftwood Community Center. It was a real treat for Billye and me. We got to see a great number of friends we had not seen in years. I was also proud to see what fine young men Tommy and Shelby had made. I knew they would. I knew their pedigree. Aside from all this the greatest thrill for me was to see the hundreds and hundreds of people pass through that community center. That whole crowd shared a common bond. That bond was the respect and affection we all have for Clarence and Edith Echols.

Think about this for a bit. If it had not been for some old coonhounds, I never would have ever gotten to know this couple. Now Son, that would have been a loss.

Rattlesnakes, Brandy, and Jack Acrey

A thing I have noticed about me and rattlesnakes is that I see the most of them during drought times. The lush times with ample rain and plant growth give rattlesnakes the necessary cover to make them difficult to be seen. They are there all right but out of sight. If rattlesnakes were one-tenth as aggressive as they are given credit for being, there would be thousands of snakebite cases each year. Most of the time Mr. Rattlesnake does business on a "you leave me alone, I'll leave you alone" basis. It is that rare encounter when the snake feels threatened that makes for the wild tales.

As I think back on half a century spent running hounds, I can only remember about five of my hounds that were bitten by rattlesnakes. Most of the time my hounds run in country that is considered to be infested with snakes. Then on the other hand I had an old friend who owned a fine-grade coonhound bitch. That little bitch was bitten nine times by rattlesnakes and ended up dying of natural causes when she was fourteen years old. A dog will usually survive a snakebite to the head. A dog bitten solidly in the body will usually die. A dog bitten during a hard race in the body is a dead dog. The exception being when the snake, for reasons known only to him, does not inject a full dose of venom with his bite.

Rattlesnakes hibernate in cold weather. In my part of the world a good portion of them use an old armadillo hole for their winter rest. They also use, particularly in rocky country, natural caves and cracks in rocks. Many times a number of them will hibernate together. I have seen rattlesnakes out and moving many times on nights when the temperature would get to freezing. I have seen rattlesnakes out and moving every month of the year. They will come out of their dens and sun around the entrance on winter days.

Rattlesnakes mate in my part of the world in the middle of the spring. The baby snakes are born alive and ready to bite and hunt in the early summer. The litters are small and would probably average seven or eight babies. The mortality rate of baby rattlesnakes is pretty high.

Rattlesnakes feed mostly on rodents. Their venom works in direct proportion to body weight. A mouse will die almost in its tracks. A rat will take a little longer. A grown rabbit may travel a distance before it dies from snakebite. Usually the snake will ambush its prey, strike it, and then trail its dying victims. A four-foot rattlesnake can swallow a fully grown cottontail rabbit easily. By the way, a rattlesnake will drink water just like a horse. He sticks his nose down in the water and sucks it up. A rattlesnake can go much longer without food than it can without water.

Newborn rattlesnakes are six or seven inches long and have a button for a rattle. The longest snake I personally have killed was an inch or two over six feet long. Most of the hundreds of rattlesnakes that I have seen were between three and five feet in length.

One drought year, 1955 I think, I collected more than two cigar boxes of rattlesnake rattles. Every snake I killed that year was killed while I followed a pack of hounds.

I have never been bitten by a rattlesnake, but I have surely had some close calls. If you want the honest truth, I am afraid of rattlesnakes.

These things I have just described to you about rattlesnakes are what, from my observation, I believe to be true. If you read some authority who gives you a different set of facts, then go with the authority. I have been known to not have seen what I thought I saw.

For a period of about fifteen years I was privileged to own and hunt two of the finest coonhounds alive during that time. They were Taylor's Black Ruby and Taylor's Black Ruby II. When Ruby II came to the end of her trail, I had no desire to go back to the woods with a coonhound. However, since hounds and hunting are as much a part of me as are food and water, I continued with a desire to run hounds. This was in 1970.

It was my opinion then that civilization was in the process of denying the foxhound and coyote-hound man a place to hunt. I, therefore, turned to rabbit hounds and beagles to satisfy my need to hunt. A cottontail rabbit in ten acres of good cover can provide fine running for a small pack of beagles, while ten miles square might not be enough country to run a coyote.

I had heard that there was to be a derby trial for beagles on the Neal Witt place below San Antonio. For purposes of this narrative it is sufficient to say that a derby is simply a young hound. I went to the trial and observed every dog that competed. My opinion was that there were only two worthwhile hounds entered, a dog and a bitch. Only the bitch interested me because I needed not only a good beagle but also one that would whelp the young dogs needed to build a pack.

The bitch's name was Brandy, and she belonged to Freddie Barbee. If memory serves, Brandy won her class that day, which made Freddie have high regards for her. He would not talk to me about selling her. A couple of weeks later Freddie ran Brandy in a trial at Bryan, and I liked her even more than I had at first. I think she placed second in her class running against all age dogs. I again tried unsuccessfully to buy her. All Freddie could talk about was running her at a trial at Waco the next weekend. If she placed at this trial, she would be qualified to run in the derby class at the Beagle International, which is held in Pennsylvania.

I did not go to the Waco trial, but late that Sunday afternoon Freddie called me and told me if I wanted Brandy I could have her for $75. I knew that Brandy had not done well at Waco. I said I would take her. Freddie told me I would have to wait a week to get her. Think he had to clear the sale with Momma? Anyway I ended up with Brandy.

Brandy was some bit better than an average beagle. Her major problem was that she could not work a straight laid set of tracks in a straight-through style. Oftentimes she would check from side to side before she would move forward. She did have one trait I considered most necessary in a hound: That characteristic was an almost fanatical determination to stay with her work and to account for the game she ran. I was probably a little harsh in my judgment of

Brandy and this was, I think, due to the quality of hounds I had run before I got her.

After I had run Brandy for about six months, I bred her back to her sire. She gave me a six-pup litter. Five of those pups were pretty plain, but the sixth one, a male, was a stem-winding dandy. There was one small problem. The pup was born with an undershot jaw. I was confident that the pup had the talent to easily earn the title of AKC Field Champion. In all honesty he was the best working beagle I have ever bred; however, I will not keep such a deformed hound, nor will I allow the possibility of that animal reproducing others of its kind. My usual practice is to destroy the animal.

A young rabbit gunner from Bryan saw the pup work, and he offered me a trade, a fair little one-eyed inbred Dooley's Rusty bitch for my pup. I agreed to the trade, provided he would accept a neutered pup. The trade was made and the pup, I think, ran out his life in a gundog pack. The little one-eyed bitch, when bred to one of George Nixon's Pearson Creek hounds, gave me two good hounds in two litters. Both had excellent licensed field-trial records.

My plan for Brandy was to continue to run her in field trials and breed her to a young hound available at that time, Wind Creek Limbo. The field trial season starts in Texas about the first of September. Brandy needed some work before the first trial.

There was a prickly pear cactus patch on Corrie Smith's place that covered about eight or ten acres. That patch was always loaded with cottontail rabbits. Billye went with me to this place one evening in the later part of August. I ran Brandy while Billye observed a family of cactus wrens. I stopped following Brandy as she worked a rabbit by my truck. Billye came into the truck and we sat on the endgate while we listened to Brandy run the rabbit. She was doing good work, especially considering the high temperature and dry conditions.

Brandy stopped giving mouth, which indicated that the rabbit had pulled some trick on her, causing her to lose contact with the trail. I knew Brandy would solve the problem because she was far too determined a hound to let a little trick played by a rabbit cause her to lose the rabbit. After a silence that lasted for several minutes, I heard her give a yipe, which was not her usual big bawl mouth. Then in a little bit Brandy came into the truck.

I knew something was wrong, so I picked her up and set her on the endgate of my truck to look her over. Sure enough, on the fleshy part of her right hind leg were a set of fang marks that oozed venom and blood. I measured the distance between the marks, almost the length of my little finger. Because of the location of this bite I knew she had little chance of survival. Nevertheless I had to try to save her.

I dropped Billye off at the house and had her instruct the vet to meet me at his office. We stood her up on his operating table, and he gave her an injection of anti-venom. I was holding her on the table, my left hand on the front of her chest, my right hand behind her rump. As the anti-venom went through her body, I felt her shudder and then she was dead.

I usually try not to let acts of nature disturb me, but poisonous snakes are my exception to this policy. As I drove home from the vet's office, I became angry at that snake for taking Brandy's life and robbing me of the pleasure of running her and her offspring. I took my hunting light, my big coon one, and hunted that snake. I looked the area over where Brandy was bitten as closely as it could be looked over at night. I found nothing. The next day Jack Acrey, an old hunting friend and a man totally at home in the woods, volunteered to help me hunt the snake.

It had rained that night. Jack and I systematically set out to cover that whole ten-acre patch. By noon we had done the best job we could. We had found seven rattlesnakes, but none of them was large enough to have fangs the width of the length of my little finger. Every one of those snakes were so well hidden that it took both a practiced eye and great determination and patience to see each one.

There is a soft spot in my heart for Brandy. She served as the vehicle to get me from coon hunting to rabbit hunting. She fell in the unenviable spot of being the replacement for the great hound, Taylor's Black Ruby II. For this reason she never received from me the credit she deserved while she was alive. I have in my pen now a fine three-dog beagle pack made up of Scruffy, Truman, and Skeeter. I raised and culled a truckload of hounds to put these three hounds together. I could drive the wheels off my truck, and the odds are that I would not find a fourth hound that could fit into this pack. Brandy could have run in this splendid little pack and made an even better pack out of it.

Good friends are ever more scarce than good hounds. Jack Acrey is a good friend. I know because he took half a day off from work to help me tromp around in a prickly pear patch looking for Brandy's killer. Jack and I have hunted together for at least thirty years. I know him well. In this day of declining morals and nonexistent loyalty, Jack casts a long shadow. If I ever had to face real trouble, I would sure do it with more confidence if I knew Jack was beside me. Yep, Jack is one of my friends.

An Antelope Hunt

In the fall of 1964 I decided to sell my interest in my business (Farm and Ranch Supply) and take a job with Texas A & M as an inspector for Texas Feed & Fertilize Control Service. On August 31, 1983, I retired from my job with Texas A & M University. I thought that fall would be a good time for me to make my first antelope hunt.

I arranged my antelope hunt to take place the first week in October. I went to Wyoming to hunt antelope. I chose to hunt the Shirley Basin out from Medicine Bow. When I got there, I spent two days studying antelope. You know, things like what they ate, when they fed, the difference between a good antelope and a run of the mill one, where they watered, when they watered, how they reacted to human pressure. I also observed the antelope hunters. I quickly lost my respect for the lot of them. They would tear across the open prairie in their vehicles, get into a group of antelope, jump out of their vehicle and start shooting as fast as they could. When the antelope got out of rifle range, they would jump back into their vehicles and look for another bunch of antelope. I did not see a hunter linger after shooting to see if he had wounded an animal. A sickening display.

I worked my little gray Chevrolet pickup across the prairie until I came to a deep gorge that had a fine little creek running through it. The sides of that ravine were so steep they stopped the passage of the antelope hunters' vehicles. My! My! I decided to make camp right there. Like to have swallowed my cud when I stepped out of my truck. I flushed a sage hen right out from under my feet. Talk about a wake-up call! But, I do know groceries when I see them, so I stalked me one of those big cocks and killed it. Dressed it, cooked it in a pressure cooker, boned it out, put it in with some rice, onions, salt and pepper, and cooked it some more in a covered pot until the rice was done. Good? *Whew*!

The Shirley Mountains start just at the south edge of the Shirley Basin. The next day I drove over to look at them. Met a Wyoming hunter who planned to elk hunt in the mountains the next day. His name was J. E. Mullens. He lived in Casper, Wyoming. That man was a hunter. I liked him. I asked him where the road into the mountains went. He said it went west up into the mountains for five or six miles where it forked off to the east. I asked where the east fork went, and he told me back out on the prairie and eventually back to where we were parked, that is if one turned left at each fork. I told him I thought I would run that loop.

He said, "Why I. T., you can't do that. That's a twenty or twenty-five mile loop."

I told him that was exactly what I was looking for.

I got my running shoes and shorts out of my truck and put them on. The temperature felt to me to be about 40°, so I also put on a light sweatshirt. It sure felt good to stretch my legs as I started up the mountains. I hit a pace that I thought would cover six miles or a tad less in an hour. I held that pace for about two hours. Man, it was almost all uphill. At the end of a couple of hours, Mr. Mullens drove up behind me. He asked if I wanted a ride back to my truck. I told him that I did not, but that I would appreciate a drink of water. After the water, I continued my run. That first couple of hours were as enjoyable as any run I ever made. Fresh beautiful mountain scenery and lots of wildlife, from chipmunks to elk. I sure was glad I was alive and where I was that morning, doing what I was doing.

Then all of a sudden it was all downhill. For me, downhill running is tough running. It uses parts of your legs that usually don't get much work. Your foot tends to work forward in the shoe and blister or bruise your toes. The downhill part only lasted an hour or so, and then I was back out on the prairie. A state employee, who was on his way to work on a campground, stopped and asked if I needed help. I told him I sure would like to have a drink of water. I must have drunk a quart of it. I thanked him and continued my run. In less than an hour I was within sight of my truck. Mr. Mullens was there at my truck.

His wife was also there. She had driven up in a motor home. Mr. Mullens told me I was going to eat lunch with them. You think I argued with him? Mrs. Mullens was a nurse in the emergency room at a hospital in Casper. I do not know how her nursing was, but her cooking was just fine.

During the meal we talked about hunting jade, hunting antelope, hunting deer, hunting elk, and Mr. Mullens talked about my run. Said he had never seen anyone run like that, and he sure had never seen an old man run the mountains. I told him that I conditioned myself so that I could do the things I really enjoyed doing the way I enjoyed doing them. I visited with Mullens until I thought maybe I had used up my welcome. Then I went back to camp.

I had a cover on the back of my pickup. In that cover I had a bed, my grub box, a gasoline stove, my old seabag full of fresh clothes, two spare tires with chains on them, and a big Styrofoam ice chest to haul my frozen antelope meat.

I made coffee, got out a folding stool, and proceeded to glass antelope and drink coffee until dark. There was a high ridge on the far side (north) of the creek that ran parallel to the creek. It was several hundred yards from the creek. I devised my plan of action. I had seen two antelope bucks that would satisfy me. The next morning I was up and had eaten a couple of hours before dawn. I took my empty backpack and my .30-06 rifle loaded with 165-grain bullets.

I crossed the creek and started working my way along and up the ridge. It was totally dark. I could only make progress by feeling my way through the sagebrush and rocks. I kept my direction by staying oriented to a set of stars I always use in wintertime to navigate by. I think they are called the Seven Sisters. In about an hour I thought I had covered about a mile. I searched for a little gully I thought I had seen on the ridge while I glassed the antelope. Most of the antelope that I saw go up or down that ridge did so within a hundred yards of that gully. In a short time I was sure I had found it. I worked my way to the top of the ridge and then came back down about seventy-five yards. It was a steep climb up and a steep climb down. I took off my backpack, sat down, and leaned up against the side of the gully. It was a shallow little wash, and I could only rest my lower back against it.

There was not a hint of a breeze blowing. The temperature felt to be around 40°. Day was just barely starting to break. It was a pure delight to sit there in the little gully while I anticipated the hunt, smelled the sage, enjoyed the nice temperature, and listened to the prairie start to wake up. In the darkness I stroked the stock of my ol' .30-06 rifle. I know by feel every scratch and scrape on it. I thanked myself for having chosen this old friend of a rifle to bring along on this hunt. Miles to the southwest I could see lights at the base of the Shirley Mountains where antelope hunters were awake and preparing for their hunt.

Finally it was light enough to see a little. I began to watch below me and west along the side of the ridge for bands of antelope. I saw none that interested me. About the time the top edge of the sun was spilling a little sunlight into Shirley Basin, I heard the rattle of hooves on loose rocks up on top of the ridge. Shortly after that I saw a doe antelope at the edge of the ridge right above me. Then one of the good bucks I had spotted the day before walked into my sight right beside the doe. I slowly raised the rifle and thumbed off the safety. With the post of the scope aligned on the bottom of the front of his chest, I increased pressure on the trigger until it broke. Recoil kept me from seeing the effect of my shot. I racked a fresh round into the chamber of my rifle as I caught the spent brass casing extracted from the chamber. This catching of the brass is an old reloader's trick. It would distress me greatly to lose a piece of brass. Anyway, I grabbed my backpack and climbed up to the top of the ridge. There my buck was. He had not moved a foot when I shot him. The shot, because the buck was standing almost straight above me, took out his heart, his lungs, and the backbone between his shoulders. It was a good shot and hardly any meat was lost.

I gutted him, tied him to my backpack, shouldered the backpack, and gathered up my rifle. As I worked down the ridge, I began to realize just how large he was. As I worked down the ridge, I could see the Mighty Antelope Hunters at work scattered across the prairie repeatedly banging away with their two-, three-, four-, five-, and six-hundred yard shots. Made me feel pretty smug about my seventy-five yard shot.

When I got into camp, I skinned my buck out. Then I boned out all the meat on a cutting board on the endgate of my pickup. Most of the hindquarters and back I cut into steaks and roasts. All the rest of the meat I ground into hamburger. I proceeded to wrap the meat in individual freezer packages. I had made a deal with the manager of the grocery store in Medicine Bow to freeze the meat for me.

Before I went back to Medicine Bow, I drove by the Mullens' motor home. Mrs. Mullens introduced me to her daughter. She had just brought in a cow elk her husband had killed. I again thanked Mrs. Mullens for the meal she had cooked for me. I asked her to convey my regards to her husband.

In Medicine Bow, I put my meat in the freezer at the grocery store. My deal was to have it out the next day, Sunday, when the store opened at noon. I then bought a bath at the hotel, followed by a fine meal at the cafe. The lady at the cafe told me I could have used her home to bathe instead of paying for a bath. She said her husband worked a night shift, so all I would have had to do was not make enough noise to wake him. I then serviced my truck. Found nice people at the service station. Went to the grocery store and bought some bread and potatoes. They were fine people at the grocery store too.

I drove out of town for a couple of miles and drove off the road for a couple of hundred yards where I made camp. I drank a little coffee, relaxed, and observed the vegetation and birds around me. Then I cleaned the bore of my ol' .30-06 rifle. Late in the afternoon I fried a package of antelope steaks and made cream gravy from the dregs. I cooked and mashed some potatoes. Cream gravy over mashed potatoes with chicken fried antelope steak made for some fine eating. Good fresh coffee makes it even better. As it got dark, I crawled into my bedroll and slept the night away.

The next morning I had coffee and then squared away all of my gear in the back of the truck. I went into town and had breakfast at the cafe. I spent the morning in the cafe sitting back out of the way, drinking coffee and eavesdropping on various conversations in the cafe. Medicine Bow is a small town. I felt the cafe had a good cross section of the town for their customers. I felt, given just a little time, I could fit into that town pretty well. I had an early lunch and was waiting when the grocery store man opened his store.

I packed my frozen antelope in the Styrofoam icebox. When I got the box in the back of my truck, I completely wrapped it in two sleeping bags. I pointed my little gray truck in the direction of Texas and let it roll. I arrived back home in San Marcos the next afternoon just after lunch. My antelope meat was still frozen, rock solid.

By the time I had finished eating that antelope, I decided the reason antelope had been hunted almost to extinction by the end of the nineteenth century was that they were easy to hunt and kill, and because they taste so good. I would have felt a lot better about my antelope hunt if the hunters I had observed had shown more respect for their obligation as hunters, and more respect for their quarry—the gallant little North American antelope. He is one fine game animal.

Still Listening

Have you ever been lonesome for a sound? I have. Expect it has been thirty-five years since I have heard it, but you know, I still catch myself listening for it.

I had heard the sound on a daily basis for almost the whole of my life, but the first time I really paid any attention to it I was lost. It was probably in the winter of 1944. I had ridden my mare to some good goose country about five miles northeast of Edna. I had gotten to the rice field in the middle of the afternoon, tied my mare at the gate, and proceeded to hunt afoot. Luck was with me, and, after a long crawl on my belly along a rice levee, I got in range of a flock of Canadian geese. I stood up and killed a good one on their rise. I continued to hunt, and as the sun started down a heavy fog settled. A flock of geese flew low over me in the increasing fog, and I was able to put a load of #2 shot in the lead goose. He started to descend out of the formation, and at the rate he was losing altitude I figured he would be on the ground before too long. I lost sight of him in the fog before he had gone too far, but I took off running as fast as I could in the exact direction in which he had disappeared. I crossed out of the rice field into open pastureland. My luck held, and in a little while I spotted him on the ground unable to fly. I ran him down and broke his neck. Then I gutted both geese. I sure felt good—two shots, two big fat Canadian geese.

I had a problem though. By this time I could not see for any distance because of the increasing fog and the descending darkness. There was no wind to get a direction from. No stars were visible in the fog for navigation. My only choice was to head out in the direction where I thought my mare was tied. I realized I was lost after I had walked for a much longer period of time than it should have taken me to get back to the rice field.

I have not been lost many times in my life, four or five are all I can remember. Be that as it may, I can tell you for sure I have had to fight off a feeling of panic and fear every time it has happened. I have to really discipline myself to keep from blindly rushing off in all directions in an effort to correct my condition.

So with a firm grip on my emotions, I slogged on into the night with the cold, the dark, the damp, and the silence. If I had fuel of any type and matches, I would have laid up for the night and tried my luck in the morning. Unfortunately, I had none of these. So it was on and on in what I knew, even at the time, was a never-ending circle. I could not even find my way back to the rice field. After a long while, my shotgun felt as if it were made of lead. I even thought about discarding the two geese because of their weight, but dropped the idea.

The cold, damp, dark and my load of a shotgun, two geese, and a pocketful of shells had maneuvered my spirits into about as low a point as teenage spirits could go. I wanted to be back home with Momma! I harangued myself for being stupid enough to get caught in such a situation. Since I had no other choice, I slogged on in the dark, the damp, the cold, and the quiet.

All at once I heard one of the most beautiful sounds I can remember, a distant train whistle from a steam locomotive—*Whoo-Ha-Whoo-Ha-Whoo-Ha-Whoo-Haaa*. Because the railroad track ran almost east and west, I instantly knew the direction to take back to my waiting mare. I headed in that direction, making the best time I could in the dark. After a while the train blew its whistle at another road crossing, and I was able to correct my direction again. In the dark I ran into the barbed-wire fence that separated the rice field from the pasture. I felt like kissing the fence. I was afraid the train would be out of my hearing before it blew its whistle again, so I followed the fence instead of cutting across the rice field and risk getting lost again. After a half-mile or so, I came to the corner of the rice field. I turned down the fence, and after a mile or so I came to a county dirt road. I headed up the road and soon I came to the gate where I had tied my mare. She nickered at me long before I got to the gate. Think she wanted to go home too. Took me all of an hour to get back home. I thought about the beautiful whistle from the steam locomotive most of the way.

I heard that sound many nights after that, some hot, some cold. Regardless of my circumstances, hunting, fishing or just camping, I always considered it a beautiful sound. The whistle from a steam locomotive is really considered to be a lonesome sound when heard at night. It is particularly lonesome when one is alone and out in the open at night. But after the night I was lost goose hunting, it was never a lonesome sound to me again. It was a comfort to me. Each time I would hear it I would feel a close relationship to the train crew, particularly the engineer and the fireman. I would feel that they were almost a part of my hunt or camp. I would have welcomed them to share a pot of camp coffee with me. I would have welcomed their stories of the trials of running a train, and I thought they would welcome my tales of hounds, fishing, or hunting. I really always felt as if I personally knew them. I sympathized with their problem of being awake while the rest of the world slept. I have always felt superior to the people who slept all night. I wondered if they shared the feeling. I felt they were my friends.

As best I can recall, it was a night in the early 1950s. Gus Eoff and I were coon hunting on the Lowman place a few miles out of San Marcos. We were about a half-mile from the railroad tracks, which were east of us. Back to the north in the direction of San Marcos, I heard a harsh, blaring, offensive sound. I asked Gus what that could possibly be. His answer was that it was a diesel train whistle and that diesel engines would replace steam. I listened as it blew for the Redwood Road crossing. I listened as it approached and blared at the College Farm Road. I listened as it blasted at the Center Point Road crossing. It made me sad to hear it. I felt as if something had been taken from me. That harsh, penetrating, intruding sound seemed to even detract from the music of the hound pack. I resented it then. I still do. Since that night I have never heard another steam locomotive whistle.

At this stage of my life I live about twenty miles southwest of the place where I got lost goose hunting. Most every evening I cast a pack of beagles on the place where I live so I can enjoy listening to them run a swamp rabbit for me. The railroad track is probably less than five miles east of my place. If the wind were in the right direction, one could hear a train whistle from the railroad track.

It would not do me any good to listen though, because the closest steam locomotive is sitting stationary in a city park in Victoria. It probably has not had up a head of steam in thirty-five years. Hell, the whistle is probably corroded up anyway. But I do listen, and you know I derive satisfaction from the listening because diesel engines do not run on that track anymore either. It is just a bare deserted railroad track. Could be all in my mind, but I feel Ol' Scruffy and Chatter and Basher sound a lot better when they run because there is no diesel train whistle to contaminate the sounds of the run.

Now, if I could just figure out a way to get them to put a steam whistle on that blamed shuttle plane that flies over my place on its route between Houston and Victoria. That would be something fine to listen to while Ol' Scruffy, Chatter, and Basher do their thing with a swamp rabbit.

Wooo-Ah-Woooo-Ah-Wooo-Ah-Wooo-Ahhh. Wouldn't that sound great with Scruffy's coarse squall, Chatter's shrill squeal, and Basher's clear bawl. Would be enough to make cold chills run up and down a man's back and might even make the hair stand up on the back of his neck. Could even keep an old man from getting lost on a foggy night.

Coffee

When I was a little kid most of the medicine I was given was in liquid form and tasted awful. This was years before the discovery of sulfa drugs, penicillin, and other antibiotics. I have a strong suspicion that the consensus of opinion was that in order for a medicine to be effective it must taste bad. Momma's antidote for the bad taste was part of a cup of black, lukewarm coffee. The coffee killed the bad taste of the medicine pretty well but it also killed my taste for coffee, particularly black, lukewarm coffee.

Back in the early 1900s the federal government had a program set up to eliminate the Texas fever tick. This program required everyone to dip his cattle in an arsenic dip every few weeks. The government saw that dipping vats were built in such a manner that no one had to drive their cattle more than three miles to get to a dipping vat. By the way, one of these old dipping vats is located on the place where I now live. During this time we lived in Ganado, and my dad had a herd of cattle about four miles east of town.

I was probably about four years old, as I remember, the first time we were required to dip our cattle. The cowboys who were to drive the cattle from our place to the dipping vat and back came to our house early for breakfast. Momma loaded the table with platters of biscuits, fried eggs, bacon, and pitchers of ribbon-cane syrup. All this food was washed down with coffee. Children were not allowed to eat at this table, but I sure stood around and watched those men wolf down Momma's good biscuits, our fresh eggs, home-cured bacon, and our fine ribbon-cane syrup.

As I remember, one of the cowboys' name was Mercer. I think maybe the Mercer family still lives around Ganado. Anyway, I remember this man as a huge man with powerful arms.

He loaded his fresh, hot coffee with cow cream and sugar, then poured a quantity of it into his saucer to cool before he slurped it down with his food.

I had never seen anyone saucer coffee before. I had never heard anyone slurping coffee before. It looked and sounded better than anything I had ever seen anyone drink. I could hardly wait until I had a chance to try it.

As soon as all the cowboys had finished eating and left, I asked Momma if I could have a cup of coffee. She poured me about half a cup. I filled the rest of the cup with cow cream and sugar in about equal proportions. Then I poured my coffee out in a saucer and slurped up a bunch of it to wash down some biscuit and syrup. Never even got to really taste it to see if it was as good as it looked and sounded. Momma's wrath came down on my head like rain in a bad storm. She informed me that we did not saucer coffee. We did not slurp coffee, and finally that we did not wash our food down with anything. Lost my taste for coffee again.

Left coffee alone until I went into the service. Then for over three years I was required to stand a four-hour watch every night on some ship, island, or station. It was the custom for everyone to drink coffee before going on watch. It helped keep you awake and alert. The cook always kept a pot of coffee ready day or night, and the last thing the cook did before going to bed was to make a fresh pot of coffee for the night watch. The whole social life of the ships and the Pacific Islands I was on revolved around the coffee pot. I learned to love it. In fact I became addicted to it. First with condensed milk and sugar, then with sugar, and finally just black coffee.

When I came out of the service, I felt I had to have coffee if I was going to fish the river at night, run hounds at night, or camp out to hunt for a while. It felt as natural to make provisions for coffee as it did for food. At that time I used an old aluminum pot that my Momma had discarded. I did not use the top to drip the coffee. I just dumped the grounds in the water and boiled them. I also, at that time, used only a campfire for cooking.

Let me interject here what I feel is the best way to make camp coffee. First get a bed of coals going from your fire, which should really be made of either oak or mesquite wood. Good camp coffee is made in a gray granite (enamel) pot. One puts a quantity of water in the pot. One then adds about a tablespoon of coffee to the pot for each cup of water. Set the cold pot of water and coffee on a bed of coals and bring the water to a rolling boil. Take the pot off the fire, pour out a cupful, and pour it back into the pot. This will settle the grounds. Then pour out a cup, set the pot close enough to the coals to keep it hot, and sit back and enjoy your wonderful brew. That first freshly brewed cup will be about as good as coffee can be, and the faint taste from the wood smoke only adds to that good taste. If it just so happens that there is a nip in the air or you have had everything go wrong all day or if your hound is leading the pack, then the cup will taste even better. An extended wet, cold camp can be a miserable experience, but good camp coffee can even offset some of that.

I have a gray granite coffee pot that I bought from an old hardware salesman, Mr. Jordan, almost forty years ago. I remember paying something less than a dollar for it. The hinge to the lid broke years ago. I wired it back on. For a long time I carried it in a cypress wood box, along with my coffee and water. Bob Winn at the State Fish Hatchery in San Marcos made that box for me. I bolted it to the running board of my pickup truck. Mine is a small pot and will hardly hold more than six cups of water. I usually make four cups at a time in it. I like to keep my coffee fairly fresh. As I think back, I can remember at least six pickup trucks that pot has outlasted. That 69¢ pot is still as good as the day it was made. Oh, there is a little enamel chipped here and there, but those only serve to remind me of special times.

When I backpack in the mountains, I do not use my fine little granite coffee pot. I have two little granite cooking pots with lids. They nestle one within the other. One holds a pint, the other a quart. They were made in Mexico. I use these to do all my backpack cooking.

Now let me tell you about real luxury. I have a little backpack gasoline stove that I use when I backpack. It is hardly larger than a can of tomatoes. I sleep under a lean-to made from a tarpaulin that will fit in my pants pocket. I sleep in a fine mummy sleeping bag. When I wake up in the morning I stick one arm out of the sleeping bag and fire up my little stove. The night before I put the required water for breakfast in each pot because the odds are all of my water will be frozen and will not pour. I set the quart pot one-half full of water on the stove and add coffee grounds. When the coffee is ready, I set the small pot that contains flaked, whole-grain cereals, raisins, and water on the fire to cook. I continue to lie in bed and sip my fresh coffee. After my cereal is ready, I add powdered milk and eat it while I reheat my coffee. After the cereal, I sip the rest of my reheated coffee. The gas stove, the little granite pots, the lean-to, the fine sleeping bag, coffee and cereal in bed . . . now, Son, that is luxury in a cold camp.

In the last fifteen or twenty years I have gotten to where I use a Coleman gasoline stove to do most of my camp cooking. I used to use my campfire as a source of light, for warmth, and for cooking. Now I seem to have better gear to keep me warm, and I seldom have a campfire for that purpose. I think I am trying to say I have gotten lazy. Anyway camp coffee cooked on a Coleman stove is almost as good as campfire coffee.

Several years ago I gave up drinking coffee. A couple of stomach disorders have dictated that I simply remove it from my life. Talk about a jolt. Man, I had a headache for three days when I stopped drinking coffee. Would take me until ten o'clock in the morning just to get started. But I finally got over my addiction.

Now I drink a substitute for coffee that is made from roasted barley, rye, chicory, and beet roots. Sort of resembles the taste of coffee—bad stale coffee—but I have gotten used to it. With a little help from my imagination, it can enhance a crisp fall night. It can make a bad day in camp seem a little better. And if my ol' hounds happen to be putting it on a hunting buddy's pack, man that imitation coffee begins to taste pretty good.

I have a couple of hunting partners, Richard Williams and J. T. Spears, who live in Lampassas. We meet every once in a while at a ranch close to Gillett to run our hounds for a few days. Richard, on special occasions, turns out some pretty fair Dutch oven biscuits for breakfast along with fried eggs, bacon, and campfire coffee.

One of these times, away out there in the brush of south Texas, I am going to take some of those biscuits, eggs, bacon, and syrup, and I am going to wash them down with saucered, cow-creamed, sugared-imitation coffee. I am going to try to make that meal sound and look as good as that cowboy breakfast did when Mr. Mercer saucered his coffee to wash down his breakfast. With a little imagination, I think I can make that imitation coffee taste as good as the real thing. It could happen!

Alone

Most of the hunting I have done in my lifetime has been done alone. In the years right after I retired (from 1983-1988) for example, I made an elk hunt, mule deer hunts, an antelope hunt, white-tailed deer hunts, squirrel hunts, rabbit hunts, and assorted bird hunts. A mental inventory confirms that I probably made more than 1,000 different hunts in this five-year period. They would range from a month backpack elk hunt to an hour's rabbit hunt with a pack of beagles. Out of all these hunts in that five years, with the exception of one dove hunt, I have hunted by myself. That dove hunt was an accident and not a planned hunt.

All of the hound men I have known when placed in circumstances where they had no hunting companion, quit hunting. They needed a hunting partner or partners to keep their interest stimulated. The same situation exists for the gun hunters I know. My opinion is that planning the next hunt with a companion, getting ready for the next hunt with a companion, and talking about a just completed hunt with a companion gives a higher sense of satisfaction to most hunters than the actual hunt. Probably in about two more generations a good number of the hunters will skip the actual hunt and just talk about it.

I am pretty sure I hunt by myself by choice. I know for certain that I do my gun hunting alone by choice. J. E. Moore was the last person I was able to gun hunt with and have total confidence in him as my partner. J. E. was a splendid pistol shot, a fine rifle shot, and more than adequate with a shotgun. The last time I saw J. E. was in 1965. He was in the process of dying of cancer. Pale, weak, and emaciated, he had somehow scrounged up a double rifle in some screwy 9mm Mauser cartridge. He had worked for weeks making the odd cartridge case used by the rifle. He had cast bullets for the rifle and had worked out loads for each barrel so that they would shoot to the same point of impact. He had that gun shooting groups of less than an inch and a half. Those groups were a combination of shots from each barrel and fired with iron sights. He had great plans for the rifle, but he was never able to make it to the woods with it. I still miss J. E. He was a hunter. He taught me much of what I know about reloading, casting bullets, and pistol shooting. He was a staunch, loyal friend.

It is strange to me that as I write stories covering a lifetime of hunting, the ones that tell the best were hunts made with someone else. My most successful hunts and my most enjoyable hunts have been hunts made alone. But I notice I do not spin many yarns about those solo hunts. My innermost feeling is that those hunts are almost too private and personal to share, and, if no one was there, then there is no one to share the hunt with.

Now with all this drivel behind me, let me tell about a hunt I once made by myself in the fall of 1980. I camped at an isolated place that I owned in the thickest of brush at a spot that is about ten yards from my present living-room window. I had two sets of beagles to run. My pack was a three-dog pack made up of three little bitches. Then I had a big beagle bitch that I ran alone. My camp consisted of a bedroll in the back of my truck and a campfire. My grub box contained sweet potatoes, Irish potatoes, onions, carrots, flour, corn meal, salt, pepper, cooking oil, and coffee. I had with me a fine little chopping ax that has been my companion for at least thirty years. I also had a good stainless S & W .357 revolver that has served me well since 1974.

If my hounds do not eat, then I do not eat. The same holds true with water. I drink only after my hounds have satisfied their thirst. I did not bring meat with me on this trip because I wanted to see how the dogs and I would fare when we had to depend on them, me, and my pistol.

The three-dog pack consisted of Alice, Jill, and Tracy. All three of these hounds were brace trial hounds and good ones. They were perfectly matched in size, speed, and ability. Each of these hounds had two wins in AKC Licensed Trials, and Alice and Jill had more than enough points to be AKC Field Champions. These were slow hounds, but they had the ability to methodically stay after a rabbit once they had him started.

I cast these three hounds to the north of my camp into thick brush, the worst of which was solid McCartney rose. They had a swamp rabbit going almost instantly. I placed myself in a likely place to intercept the rabbit as my pack pursued him in their slow methodical style. After about a fifteen-minute wait, I spotted Mr. Swamper creeping through the McCartney rose. My pistol was loaded with a mild .38 special load, and I was able to make a head shot on the rabbit at a distance of less than six feet. I gutted the rabbit, retaining all his vital organs. In a two-hour period I was able to repeat that process three more times. The only variation was the distance of the shot.

I picked up the pack and went into camp. There I finished dressing the four rabbits. I put all the vital organs—the hearts, lungs, kidneys and livers—in an aluminum bucket and boiled them in a little water. Three of the rabbits I laid out on a wire grill over some oak coals. That took care of the preparation of dog food.

For my supper I chose an Irish potato, sweet potato, and an onion. I washed each of them, oiled the outside of each lightly, added a little salt and pepper to the onion, wrapped each vegetable in aluminum foil, and placed them on the grill over the coals. I took the whole carcass of the best rabbit, oiled it lightly, sprinkled on salt and pepper, wrapped it in foil, and added it to the food on the grill. I put on a pot of coffee, and that took care of the human food. All it needed was a turning and a waiting.

I broke open the cooked Irish potato, mashed up its insides, added a little salt and pepper, and poured the juice from the cooked rabbit package over the smashed-up potato. I opened the onion package and poured the dark brown juice from the well-done onion over the potato. I then proceeded to enjoy a meal that I consider gourmet cooking at its best. Dessert was the sweet potato washed down with good, freshly brewed camp coffee. Hot damn!

As dark settled in and to an ever-resounding chorus of owls hooting, I cast Vickie. Vickie was not a field-trial hound. Vickie was a rabbit shagger. She would get up on an old swamp rabbit and make him sail. She had enough ability to stay up on that rabbit once she jumped him. What I am trying to say is that if that rabbit did not get up and move, then he was a caught rabbit. Vickie had a bad fault that I tolerated. She would not run with another hound. She did her own thing in her own way and that is the only way she would do it. I really did not tolerate Vickie. Hell! I loved her. By herself, doing her own thing, she would catch more rabbits than any beagle I have ever hunted. She gave you a beautiful, exciting, melodious race while she did this.

Vickie scooted out of camp about fifty yards and started a rabbit. That rabbit chose to make his race around and around my camp, never more than a hundred yards from where I sat drinking coffee. After about an hour and in spite of the thick brush, I could tell that the rabbit was weakening. I stepped out and caught Vickie.

It was then suppertime for the hounds. Their meal consisted of boiled rabbit vital organs and rabbit barbecue. They seemed to consider it gourmet cooking too.

After feeding the hounds, I left camp with a small flashlight, a varmint call, and my pistol. I went to an earthen tank about two hundred yards from camp. I showered down on my varmint call, and in only a few seconds a boar coon responded. I speared him with the beam of light in my left hand as I centered him in the sights of my pistol in my right hand. The shot hit him at the base of his neck and angled into his body cavity from between his shoulders. He fell in his tracks. He was a good-sized boar coon, and I thought he would weigh at least twelve pounds.

I dressed him, and in camp I put his vital organs in my boiling bucket and his carcass on the wire grill. I was happy. I had dog food for at least two days. I stirred up my fire, warmed up a last cup of coffee, and, since I seldom stay up in camp after dark, I turned in.

It would have been a great pleasure to have turned my pack aloose to run all night. I would have enjoyed listening all during the night. I have a rule, though, that I do not leave my hounds to run unsupervised. That is a good way to get crossways with your neighbors, and angry landowners are things hound men already have too many of. It is also a good way to lose a hound.

I was up before daylight the next morning. In short order I stirred up the fire and made fresh coffee. Then I added boiling water and a little salt to some cornmeal, adding just enough water to make a thick paste. I dropped spoonfuls of this mixture into a frying pan of hot cooking oil. I left it long enough to brown all over and took it out. It sure went good with fresh coffee and a few slivers from the coon. I knew where there was a bee tree, and I was tempted to go cut it in order to have honey to go with my hot water cornbread. I scrapped the idea because I just was not prepared to handle honey.

The back border of my place is Arenosa Creek. It is about ¾ of a mile from where I was camped. I left the dogs in camp, and by good daylight I was on the creek looking over hickory-nut trees for squirrels. Between squirrels eating hickory nuts and squirrels eating acorns, I killed a good mess of squirrels that morning. I do not remember the exact number of pistol bullets it took to kill the squirrels. If I made a guess I would have to either lie or embarrass myself to come up with a figure. Let's just say I used enough bullets to get four squirrels—okay?

Back in camp I fried up the squirrels. The bony pieces of the front half of the squirrels I added to carrots, potatoes, and onions and cooked them into a stew. The meaty hind parts I fried for lunch with fried potatoes. I saved enough of the good pieces to do for breakfast.

While I was squirrel hunting, I observed a good deal of gray fox signs. In the middle of the afternoon I took Alice and my varmint call and went about half a mile north of camp. I blew the call, and it was not long before I caught the movement of a fox in the brush. Alice opened on the fox as soon as she got his scent. She had run a fox before. I left her running and returned to camp. Tracy was faunching to go to Alice, so I cut her loose first. As soon as I heard Tracy put in with Alice, I turned Jill aloose and I left camp and went to the running pack.

I followed the pack for an hour or so. They moved a fox at a faster pace than they did a rabbit; a fast walk with an occasional trot would keep me right on top of them. A fox leaves more scent than a rabbit and is, therefore, easier to run. Those little bitches had complete control of the line, and they worked it in a beautiful fashion.

Several times I saw where the fox had made an abrupt turn. The lead hound would run over the line. In every case I saw the second hound make the turn, while the lead hound fell in at the back of the pack. In the time I stayed on top of the pack, I never saw a hound separated by more than a couple of feet from the pack. Every hound served as lead hound, second hound, and rear hound. I could have picked up any hound or any two hounds and the race would have continued just as well at the same pace. Alice, Jill, and Tracy were fine little hounds.

I left them running until an hour or so after good dark. Due to the slow pace of the pack and the thick brush, that fox did not run too far from where he was started. As far as I know he only left my place once and that was a couple of hundred yards loop through the place to the east of me. Those little bitches did like to run a fox, and I had to drag them out of the woods.

In camp it was fresh coffee and squirrel stew for me and roast coon for the dogs. From the actions of the hounds I got the idea that the coon was fully as good as the squirrel. I did not worry about it though because I was in my bedroll and asleep to the tune of the dogs crunching on coon bones.

The next morning I made breakfast of cold, fried squirrel and fried, hot-water cornbread all washed down with freshly brewed camp coffee. As I leaned back with my last cup of coffee and warmed myself beside my campfire, I realized that all was right with my world.

I had burned up all the fallen dead limbs in the general area of camp, so I decided to use the morning to gather wood. I found a dead blackjack oak tree about a hundred yards northwest of camp. I chopped that tree up into pieces that I could just barely drag and carry. I ended up with a big stack of the best campfire wood on the face of this earth. I piled up enough to do for a future hunt.

I built the fire up and turned Vickie aloose. Pistol shooting a rabbit in front of Vickie was harder than shooting one in front of my pack. Vickie did not allow Mr. Swamper to creep around. She made him run. Be that as it may, twenty minutes and a couple of shots later I had a swamp rabbit for lunch. I dressed him, rolled him in flour, fried him, made gravy out of the dregs, put the gravy and the fried rabbit along with some chopped onions, salt and pepper in a covered cast-iron pot and let it simmer till I could not wait any longer. The meat was so tender it was falling off the bone and was it good! I made myself save about a fourth of it for supper.

Loafing in camp seemed the thing to do, so I did it for the afternoon. For supper I cooked three big sweet potatoes. I ate two of them with smothered rabbit poured over them. The third potato I saved for breakfast.

As it began to get dark, I cast my pack and let them run for a couple of hours. I caught them off, fed the last of the coon to the hounds, and crawled in bed.

Early the next morning after a breakfast of leftover sweet potato and coffee (don't knock it till you try it) I tried unsuccessfully to call another coon. As I walked back to camp, I spotted an armadillo. I always wanted to eat an armadillo anyway, so I shot him. I hung him up off a tree limb and started dressing him. A couple of hours later I gave up in frustration. I could not dress that armadillo and have him in a condition I would eat. I took my chopping ax and chopped him up into pieces. I cooked him hide, hair, shell, and all over the coals for the dogs. I still never have eaten an armadillo, but one of these days I plan to try to dress one again.

I ate hot-water cornbread and coffee for lunch. Meat for the dogs was not a problem, but meat for me was. I spent the whole afternoon squirrel hunting. I only killed two. I fried them for supper and ate them with baked potato and baked onion. The hounds enjoyed armadillo as much as they had coon.

Early the next morning I cast my pack as I fried hot-water cornbread to go with leftover fried squirrel. They started the rabbit that wanted to run circles around camp. I sat back, drank coffee, and let them run for at least three hours. I picked them up and cast Vickie. After Vickie had punished a rabbit for an hour or so, I caught her up. It was time to break camp.

I cleaned up camp, rolled up my bedroll, loaded the dog box, the grub box, and the hounds. It was a twelve-mile drive to the closest town. I thought the whole way about what to have for lunch. Finally decided that a can of sardines, some crackers, and an onion would be just what I wanted. People in that grocery store sure acted funny.

They looked at me a lot and gave me an abundance of room. Never thought too much of it until I got home. Billye told me I smelled like a combination of wet dog, a wild varmint, a wood fire, and a dirty old man. She said I looked horrible too—unshaven, unwashed, uncombed, and dressed in filthy clothes. I sure did feel good.

That was just an ordinary hunt, but it caused a dramatic change in my life. It made me realize that I had worked for a living about long enough and that I had lived in a congested, expanding urban area for far too long. I set a number of goals for myself, and within three years I had retired from my job. Within another three years my old home had been sold and my new home had been built on the west side of the tree I had camped under. Alice, Jill, Tracy, and Vickie are gone to where old dogs go. They were replaced by a dandy pack made up of Skeeter, Scruffy, and Truman. My new neighbors are deer, coyotes, foxes, bobcats, coons, squirrels, rabbits, wild ducks, wild turkeys, doves, owls, crows, a creek, and tankful of fish.

I hunt something most every day, and, like Ol' Vickie, I mostly do it my way, alone.

A Saturday Night Special

In the fall of 1964 I started work on a job that required I be away from home. At that time I owned a little Ruger Bearcat pistol. I had a machinist fit the adjustable rear sight from a S & W Kit gun to this gun and he put a ramp post front sight on it. I used this pistol mostly to shoot coons out of trees after my hounds treed them. With the adjustable sight and a reworked trigger, it turned out to be a handy, efficient little tool. I would leave this pistol at home when I traveled so that Billye would have a protective firearm in the house. Billye shot this pistol well.

In 1966 we moved from Amarillo to Beeville. I did a lot of dove hunting around Beeville, and one of my hunting companions was the manager of the Penny's store there. The only name I remember for him is Tate, though I cannot remember whether that is a first or last name. Anyway, Tate saw this little worked-over Bearcat pistol one day and apparently fell in love with it. He pestered me for months trying to buy it. Finally he got his offering price up so high that I took him up on it. I probably got $40 for it.

A few days after I sold the Bearcat, I was in Wharton. That afternoon after work I went to Carrol's Gun Shop. There I found a used S & W Kit gun with a 2" barrel and square grips. After some long, drawn-out haggling, I ended up buying it from Donny Carrol for $45. It was a fine little gun and in almost new condition. I used it as I had the Bearcat, to shoot treed coons and a house gun for Billye.

Smith and Wesson came out with a stainless steel pistol. It was on their smallest frame, the same frame as the Kit Gun. It had a 2" barrel and round grips. It was in .38 caliber and is about as small as a .38 caliber revolver can be made. It was named the Model 60.

The pistol had been on the market for several years but was rather expensive and in short supply. Few of them ever appeared on the used-gun market. I met a young man at Belton who had one he wanted to get rid of. His last name was Whiteside. This would be in 1973. I traded him a nice Remington M722 rifle in .308 caliber for this pistol. I probably had to throw in some boot.

After a weekend spent searching for a load that was both accurate and shot to the point of aim, I found a load using one of my 155-grain HP cast bullets that performed very well. I was about 45 years old at this time and my eyes and eye-hand coordination enabled me to get almost the full potential from a pistol and loaded round combination. With this pistol and my best load for it, I could hold 98 percent of my shots in a $3^{4}/_{10}$-inch circle at 25 yards shooting offhand.

By the time I had acquired this Model 60 pistol, I had quit coon hunting. So I sold the little S & W Kit gun and hung the Model 60 on a deer horn at the head of my bed for Billye to use as a house gun.

I started running rabbits with beagles after I quit coon hunting. A fact of life is that cottontails and rattlesnakes live in the same kind of country. Two things bothered me: First my beagles were getting bitten by rattlesnakes, and second it seemed I was forever running into a rattlesnake at the most inopportune moment. I started working with shot loads in pistols in order to be able to effectively dispatch those rattlesnakes that needed dispatching. I started with .38 caliber loads and shot them in all barrel lengths from $8^{3}/_{8}$" to 4". I discovered that the shorter the barrel the better it handled shot shells. Following this concept to its logical conclusion, I got the little 2" barrel Model 60 down and tried shot shells in it. The results were excellent.

The problem with these loads was that past six feet the pattern with No. 9 shot was so sparse that one could not depend on hitting a rattlesnake with it. Number 9 shot was the smallest shot size available. I discussed this problem with an old friend, Don Miller, one Sunday morning over coffee. His solution was to use No. 12 shot. I explained that there was no No. 12 shot available. Don went to a storage cabinet and after a little searching tossed me a sack that contained about four pounds of No. 12 shot. Because of the beautiful relation we shared, I did not offer to pay for the shot. I knew that at some time in the future Don would need some shooting accessory and that I would supply it. Don and I have carried on this arrangement for almost thirty years. I am willing to bet that if we had kept books on our transactions that they would show that we are about dead even with each other after thirty years.

The No. 12 shot worked to perfection in the Model 60 pistol. At fifteen feet it would hold every shot on a 8½" x 8½" square paper. The pattern was so dense that a small earthworm would have been hit by it. That No. 12 shot in the Model 60 was simply double purple poison to a rattlesnake. Rattlesnakes hit while on a hard surface like rock, pavement, or a floor were blown into the air and away for a foot or so. Those shot on a soft surface seldom if ever moved when hit. In either instance it was instant death. I took to carrying the Model 60 every time I hunted my beagles.

Since I had the little Model 60 with me most of the time I hunted, I used it a good deal for things other than snakes. For instance, using regular cast bullets, I have used it to kill several cottontail rabbits when I needed one to eat in camp. I can also remember at least two messes of quail I killed with this little .38 pistol and cast bullets. I can remember one fox squirrel I killed with the gun. But I must confess that the combination of the Model 60 plus my cast bullets and my aging eyes have all added up to a pretty poor kill-ratio on fox squirrels. I killed one doe white-tailed deer with a single shot through the rib cage from a distance of about twenty yards. That doe ran about twenty yards before she went down. My varmint kills with the gun include a number of coons, a fox, several nutria, two gone-wild house cats, and possibly other varmints that do not come to mind. I have used it to shoot at a few coyotes. To the best of my knowledge I have never hit a coyote with it. All the coyote shots have been rather long ones at moving targets.

So all in all my little Model 60 S & W has been a most satisfactory firearm for me. Using shot shells, it performs in a most excellent fashion on rattlesnakes, copperheads, and cottonmouths. It has supplied me with food on several occasions when I needed meat in camp. It is small, light, and easy to carry. For this reason it is with me when I need it more than a larger, heavier pistol would be. It is a joy to keep clean because the stainless steel feature makes it easy to deter rust. Its presence has been a comfort for Billye many times over the years, and its presence has given me a sense of security in several situations as well. So through the years it has served me well as both a hunting arm and a security gun.

There is a group of people in our society who looks at my little Model 60 S & W with a different point of view. The expressed aim of these people has been to register firearms, ban the sale of pistols, ban the sale of firearms, ban so-called assault rifles, and to make all firearms less accessible to the American public. They have a catch name for small handguns, cheap handguns, or short-barrel handguns; they call these "Saturday Night Specials." The premise of their vociferous outpouring over "Saturday Night Specials" has been that these guns serve no other purpose than to kill hapless humans. My little Model 60 S & W is a prime example of what these people call a Saturday Night Special. The daily broadcasts from these people, by all forms of news media, propounded the theory that these pistols had no sporting adaptions at all. My! My!

I have never owned an assault rifle. The U. S. Government taught me to shoot one though, a big clumsy thing called a Garand rifle. I would not give you a plugged nickel for any semiautomatic rifle if I had to keep it and use it. Be that as it may, I know an ol' boy who does not live too far from me. He farms rice. Wild hogs are attracted to the rice grain and the water used to grow it. In order to raise a crop successfully, this man must control these wild hogs. He tells me the most efficient tool available for this control job is an assault rifle. Several times I have seen him with a whole pickup load of from twelve to eighteen dead hogs that he had killed in his rice field. By the way, none of the meat from these animals is wasted. Most of it goes where it does the most good. Now the gun-control people tell you that these assault rifles are only used by criminals, particularly drug criminals. That assault rifles have no sporting adaption at all. It would be pretty hard to sell that concept to my rice-farming friend. I would bet I could find five more adaptions of assault rifle to sporting or work-related uses within twenty miles of me.

Anyway I am most thankful that the gun-control people have as yet been unsuccessful in their efforts to make handguns unaccessible to me. I am also thankful that they have not been successful in banning rifles and shotguns from me too.

Now let me tell you the story of my Model 60 pistol from 1984 to 1990. This is a painful story, but please bear with me. I lived in San Marcos in 1984, and at the last of March that year my youngest son, Wade, who was twenty-eight then came by the house for a visit. Billye was working at that time, so Wade and I had the house to ourselves. We had a good visit. I made coffee and we shared the pot. After a couple of hours, Wade said that he planned to meet a couple of friends for lunch so he would not stay for lunch with me. He had come to the house afoot, so as he started to leave I asked if I could take him anywhere. His answer was that he preferred to walk for the pleasure of it as he had been cooped up in an office for far too long.

He waved at me as he left, and I never saw him again. Two days later a friend of his called from Austin and told me that Wade had not been to his apartment for at least two days. Then the next day, Sunday, I discovered my little Model 60 Pistol was missing from its place over my bed. My mind played over a thousand scenarios, none of which had pleasant endings. I filed a missing-persons report with the Austin Police Department (Wade's home) and my Hays County Sheriff. I realized one day soon after that I would never see Wade again. You see he knew me well. He knew from experience that one could steal much of my personal property like money, tools, or equipment, and I would only get upset enough to batter the person a little. That I would only search for such a person for a few years. But the person who steals one of my firearms or one of my hounds, now that is a different matter. That person has invaded a part of me that I do not allow to be invaded. I would never stop searching for that son-of-a-bitch, and I would make no effort to control my fury when I do find him. Wade knew these things.

Time passed with no word of Wade. In the meantime I moved from San Marcos to Edna. The uncertainty of the situation never gave me any peace of mind. The horror of it all invaded my mind during my waking hours, and it dominated my mind during sleep. Then the local sheriff's department contacted me in January of 1989. They informed me that Wade's remains had been found. The police department in San Marcos informed me that he had been found in a thick brush-covered lot in the city limits of San Marcos. This lot was six blocks from my old home. He had taken his own life with my Model 60 pistol, using one of my cast bullets in one of my handloads.

There are many details to be attended to in a situation like this. One of the last ones was to meet with the detective in charge of the case. He related to Billye and me all the details he had about the case. He then brought into his office all the items found at the death site. All of these things had been exposed to the weather for four years, so all were in poor condition. The natural fibers of clothing had rotted away, leaving a zipper and buttons. There were parts of his shoes. His little backpack was there. The synthetic material was still in fair shape. There was a notebook, the contents of which were destroyed by the elements. There were some coins and a billfold of synthetic material that contained driver's license, some paper money, and the usual clutter found in billfolds. The billfold and its contents were in surprisingly good condition. Finally there was my Model 60 pistol. The leather holster had rotted. The wooden grips had decayed. The stainless steel showed a good deal of corrosion because of the exposure to blood, body fluids, and the elements.

I accepted all of these items from the police department. I brought them home. I went through them one by one. As I examined an item, I put it into a garbage bag: the buttons, the zipper, the shoes, the backpack, the notebook, the billfold and its contents, except for the money. I also held back the pistol. I took the garbage bag and placed it in a dumpster. The money I placed in a little clear plastic bag. I set a trap with it. There is a young retarded man in Edna who helps support himself and his mother with the proceeds of aluminum cans he picks up and sells. I tied the plastic bag of money to an empty aluminum can. Then I put that can with five others in a pile in a location that I knew this young man worked. I hope he enjoyed his find.

The Model 60 I looked at for several days. The whole working mechanism of the pistol was frozen by corrosion. I discovered that the trigger and hammer of this pistol were not stainless steel. They were almost rusted away. I scrubbed the gun in water. Then soaked it in penetrating oil. I beat the hammer back. I beat the cylinder latch back. I hammered the cylinder open. I removed the four loaded rounds and the spent round. I ran a wire brush and solvent through the cylinders and barrel. Much to my amazement I found the bore and the chamber in perfect condition.

Understand I did not need another Model 60. You see I had bought one shortly after Wade took my first one because I found it to be too useful for me to be without one. I gave $200 for the new used one. I sent the corroded pistol to S & W. They sent me an estimate of $225 to repair it. I instructed them to repair the gun. They had to replace everything except the barrel, the cylinder, and the frame. When I received it back from the factory I compared the accuracy of the two Model 60s. The old repaired pistol outshoots the new pistol in every way, shot shells or cast bullets; long distance or close. I traded the replacement pistol off shortly after that.

Since I received it back from the factory I have used my little Model 60 a great deal. I have killed at least a half-dozen rattlesnakes, some with shot shells and some with cast bullets. I have also killed many copperheads here on the place. I have killed a bunch of cottonmouths in this period. I turned down an opportunity to kill a javelina with it from a distance of about six feet. He left my dogs alone; I left him alone. So as you can see, my Model 60 is back to doing what it does best; being accurate, reliable, and available.

I have no real information about the things that could have tormented Wade to the point that he would choose to take his own life. He kept those things well hidden from me. I have no idea why he would choose to use my gun for that purpose. I do know that he knew I only keep the best of good guns and that my handloads for each of my guns will perform better than any ammunition offered for sale anywhere.

In my lifetime out of all the hundreds of guns I have owned, there are only three that are special to me, a .30-06 rifle, a 20-gauge shotgun, and a .44 Magnum pistol. These are the only guns I own that I will not sell or trade. I will use them as long as my health and our laws allow. Since I got my Model 60 back from the factory, I have developed a special feeling for it. It would seem natural that a parent would feel revulsion for the instrument that was used to kill his son, but I do not have that feeling. Instead I feel that it is my last link with Wade.

Instead of remembering the horror of what the pistol was used to do, when I pick up the pistol to use it, I remember back to the many good times Wade and I shared. Like the time he and I walked down the hill from our house one night to Purgatory Creek. I blew the varmint call and worked the light. I called in a huge boar coon. Wade shot him square dab in his open mouth from about four feet. We could not find an exit hole from the bullet. He used my little Model 60 and a cast bullet. The coon reared up and fell dead. I had Wade pitch it in Dick Drysdale's yard where he kept his two basset hounds. Ol' Dick bragged for a year about the big boar coon his bassets killed. Wade and I never mentioned what we had done with the coon. Wade thought it was even funnier because only he and I knew. So did I.

I do not hold my M60 responsible for Wade's death. The forces that ended the life of my son go beyond the owning of a firearm. I do know that gun control would not have played a role in changing the events that happened. I have no doubt that when Wade made his decision to take his life he would have done so even if there were no guns on this earth. The cause or causes of Wade's death were social problems. Most of the problems we face today are social problems—pollution, energy, education, poverty, drugs, crime, illegal aliens, and health care, to name a few. We have had little success in controlling these social problems with legislation. I strongly believe that we will never control the social problems or the misuse of guns by legislation either.

Water, Lonely, and Lightning

Space and weight in my backpack were precious. Shelter, clothing, food, cooking utensils, plus sundry necessities were carefully selected and packed. Then I chose a book written by one of my heroes, Roy Bedichek, to read in my leisure time. I also chose to give the space and weight to a spiral notebook so that I could write down thoughts and experiences that came to me during this adventure. This extended backpack trip into a wilderness area was to be the culmination of a lifelong dream to make such a trip. There was the additional motive on my part of letting Nature heal some of the wounds inflicted by a heavy buildup of stress from a complex and difficult work situation. I have used Nature as my security blanket for physical and emotional stress since early childhood, having learned early on that when my problems became a heavy weight to carry, a few moments observing tadpoles or doodlebugs could quickly prepare me to go back and work out my problems with renewed energy. My therapeutic use of Nature can be as casual as a short walk down the hill from my house or it may be as complex as the month-long backpack trip planned for a wilderness area in Idaho. No matter the occasion, Nature has never disappointed me with what she has to offer. My backpack trip was no exception, and I would like to share with you some of the things I wrote in my notebook during the first week of my trip. Since each of these experiences is, I feel, unique, I have given them names so that you can more easily follow me from one to another. I call them Water, Lonely, and Lightning.

Water

We take many of the things in our daily lives for granted. We walk up to a fountain and take a drink of water. We go to the kitchen and run water to prepare a meal. We go the bathroom and draw water for a bath. Most of us never really think about water.

Have you ever tasted cold, clear, sparkling, mountain spring water? Have you ever had the luxury of the finding of a source of drinking water being your most important problem?

I was camped near Nelson Point in Idaho. Nelson Point is a geographic location, not a town. I was about out of water. In fact I had used the last I had making coffee for breakfast. I broke camp and found a trail that led down into a valley. I followed the trail for half a mile or so where I found a stream crossing the trail. I followed the stream up the mountain to its source. There I found a tiny spring bubbling out of the rocks. I cleared the vegetation and moved the dirt from its mouth. The steady flow of water quickly cleared the mess I had made. I took a cup of it to drink. Cold! Do you remember how cold ice cream was when you were a kid? Made your head hurt. Five swallows and my head hurt. I took another cup and drank it. A marmot up on the side of the mountain whistled at me. I rolled over in the grass and grinned at him. Oh ho! My last big problem of the day solved.

My feeling of well-being was short-lived though. As I lay in the grass I remembered back to the time I was a teenage boy roaming the river bottoms in the Coastal Bend area of Texas. When I was thirsty, I would lie down and drink from the flowing river water. It was then as clear and pure as Idaho spring water. I remembered back to a later time when my children were youngsters. Our family would camp on a Central Texas Hill Country creek or river for days at a time. When drinking water was needed, I would send one of the boys down to the stream to get a bucketful. It was then as clear and pure as Idaho spring water. Today all of this water is contaminated with industrial waste, agricultural waste, and human waste to the point that it is not fit for consumption. My last big problem of the day may have been solved, but you and I have a bigger problem yet to be solved. Eventually the finding of a source of drinking water will be our most important problem. The solving of this problem will not be a luxury, as it was for me in an Idaho wilderness.

Lonely

Standing alone on the top of a ridge in Idaho I could look in four directions and see as far as I could walk in days. To the best of my knowledge, there was no one in any of this country. It was a lonely experience.

Yesterday I walked down a trail in a snowstorm. Snow limited visibility to some fifty yards. I came to a place where snow-covered trees formed a room with me in the middle. I stood there for some time. I could not hear a sound. There was no one within miles of me. That was a lonely experience.

For the past twenty years I have had to, as a part of earning a living, spend a number of nights most weeks in some motel room. One may be near many people while in a motel, but, at best, it is still a lonely experience.

I have been to parties where many people were gathered to have a good time. Conversations flowed like chatter from tree squirrels. I have gone for a whole evening and never heard a sincere thought expressed. It is a lonely experience.

A couple of months ago my problems built up to the point that I spent a restless night worrying about them. The next morning, as we lay in bed enjoying our morning coffee, I tried to share these problems with my wife. Her own problems were so compelling that she hardly heard a word I said. That is a lonely feeling.

To me to be motel lonely, or party lonely, or lonely with loved ones is terrible. I have observed each of them with my friends, and I have seen these friends destroyed in a slow insidious manner.

To me wilderness lonely is beautiful. It sets my mind to racing. It makes me remember the beautiful things of my life: my wife, my family, my friends. It lets me get the beautiful things of my life in proper perspective. It inspires me to be a better person.

I have observed that people are constantly concerned with the economics of the world, the use of atomic power, the threat of war. Personally, I am optimistic that we will resolve or work our way through these problems. My fervent hope is that my grandchildren will have a place to go to be lonely. That such a place in a wilderness will be left for their use.

I hear people say, "Have a good day." I think a far better phrase would be, "HAVE A GOOD LONELY."

Lightning

My mother had a fear of lightning. I remember her telling me that a bolt of lightning had struck in front of the house as she stood and watched a storm from the front door. The lightning bolt knocked her unconscious. This happened before I was born. From her as a child I also learned to fear lightning. I can never remember being comfortable during an electrical storm, whether I was by myself, with someone, in a house, or in any other circumstances.

In 1973 I drove from San Marcos, Texas, to Pittsburgh, Pennsylvania, to run a beagle bitch named Crooked in the Beagle Derby International. The brace just ahead of Crooked and me was running on top of a hill. A bolt of lightning hit somewhere between that hilltop and the clubhouse. When it hit, Ol' Crooked jumped straight up into the air. She was the quickest, but I was the strongest because I passed her at about four feet. I noticed the judges got down off their horses, and the gallery came to where I was in the valley after the bolt. Ol' Crooked and I were put down to run right after that. Neither of us was in any shape to make a decent go of it.

One Sunday morning I was in the woods a mile or so from my house. I was working with a couple of hound pups. A thunderstorm boiled up and formed right over my head. My youngest son was visiting at the house, and my wife was dressing for church. My son said how he hated for me to be caught out in the storm. My wife told him not to worry. That I would not be out in the storm for long. I am a slow, old man but I can be inspired to my best effort by lightning. My wife told me later that I was back at the house putting the pups in their run before she could finish her comment.

I was camped in a wilderness area in Idaho, with a canvas lean-to stretched between two trees as my camp home. I was asleep on the ground. A thunderstorm came up. This was not an imitation thunderstorm. It was not a puny, little, old Texas thunderstorm. Believe me, it was a full-grown, Idaho slambanger of a thunderstorm. The closest house to me was at Warren, Idaho, some nine miles as the crow flies. No crows were flying that night. My truck was almost that far away. No place to go. Nothing but stark fear to keep me company.

Got to watching the blamed thing and discovered that it was downright beautiful as well as fascinating. Some of the flashes lit up the sky and seemed to just flash up in the sky horizontal to the ground. Others seemed to extend from the sky to the earth and had definite bolt shapes. Mountain thunder cannot compare to prairie thunder, but this thunder did pretty well.

About the time I was starting to enjoy myself, a bolt hit a tree not a hundred yards from my bed. Before I could get back down to the ground, another one hit even closer. Ho boy! Thunder crawled in my bedroll with me.

I wished, as I lay in my bedroll, that I could talk to my Momma. I would have told her that she should have been careful about what she taught me as a child. That her teachings would be with me more than half a century later. Then I got to thinking. You know, Momma was careful in what she taught me. I never have had a problem distinguishing between right and wrong. She taught me that. She taught me to love, to work, to save, to be good to my word, to be proud, to be loyal, to stand for my beliefs, to share, to assume responsibility, and how to be a parent. She taught me these things by example. By example she showed me how to live. By example she also showed me how to die.

You know, a fear of lightning is not much of a price to have paid to have the privilege of growing up as a part of this woman's family.

Come on Mother Nature, try me again. Momma and I will try to be ready for you next time.

A day or so after the thunderstorm, the weather turned bad. I was quickly up to my limit in snow and down to my limit in temperature. I learned a lot about myself. I had quite a number of beautiful experiences after that, but I discovered an interesting thing. Reading and writing are luxuries. The necessity to meet my daily needs for shelter, food, and warmth took those luxuries from me. I reached the point where given the choice of writing down an experience or using the paper to start a fire with wet wood was really no choice at all. I chose the fire every time. Roy Bedichek, the author of the book I had with me, was a naturalist. I eased my conscience by telling myself he would have understood why I burned his book. I discovered that the promise of a hot pot of tea at the end of a day could be more of a motivating factor than all the monetary gain dangled before me in my working life. A racking experience with hypothermia showed me just how precious my life was to me. As I said, I learned a lot about myself.

Nevertheless, Nature sent me out of her wilderness with my body lean and fit and my mind equally lean and fit. It was a wonderful feeling to have reached an understanding about myself on Nature's terms. Nature's challenges left me eager to confront the very problems that had so battered me in the past. I was never more happy to be alive. I was never more happy that I still had a part of my life to live.

One day I plan to return to that wilderness area. I hope I can find a place to be lonely; I hope I can experience another thunderstorm. However, I cannot go back too soon. It is sort of like drinking cold, mountain spring water. I just cannot take too many swallows too quickly.

565275

If I had to limit my ownership of guns to one gun, it would be an easy decision. For me the story of this gun started in 1964. In the fall of 1964 I could see a little daylight at the end of a long, narrow tunnel. I had sold out my interest in a farm and ranch supply business. I had just sold my house for more than I thought possible for it to bring. The house sold so easily in a tough market that old friend John Smith would accept only a token commission for the sale. I had taken a job with Texas A&M University as an inspector for Texas Feed & Fertilize Control Service. I was a few dollars ahead for the first time in my life.

For years I had wanted a first-class .30-06 rifle but could never afford it. As we were preparing to move to our new home in Amarillo, I asked Billye if she thought our improved financial situation would warrant the purchase of such a rifle. Her answer was that she thought I should get exactly the rifle I wanted.

In all my dreams, thoughts, and slobbering over a rifle, I had never considered any rifle except a Winchester Model 70 in .30-06 caliber. Wouldn't you know just about the time I could finally afford such a rifle, Winchester quit making the Model 70 I wanted. In its place they started producing a new Model 70, which I did not want.

Early in 1965 I met a hunter in Clovis, New Mexico, who had the Winchester model I wanted. He was in the process of having a custom rifle built, and he needed cash to pay for it. I bought his pre-World War II Model 70, .30-06 for $90.00. I put Weaver bases and rings on it to hold a K4 Weaver scope, and I was in business. My only problem was that the gun would absolutely not shoot good groups.

I spotted a really clean, used, featherweight, Model 70 .30-06 at Amarillo Gun Traders. It took a whole Saturday morning to complete the transaction, but I ended up with the featherweight on an even trade.

Much to my dismay, this rifle would not shoot well either. There was a small gun shop, whose name I can't remember, a few blocks from Amarillo Gun Traders. I was able to trade my featherweight for another featherweight as an even trade. I could hardly believe my luck when I discovered that it would not shoot decent groups either.

Late in 1966 I noticed a Numerich Arms ad in *The American Rifleman* for a new standard Model 70 .30-06 barrel for $26. I ordered one. About that time I moved to Beeville, Texas. I had Bryan Dugat of Beeville change out barrels for me. The new barrel was stamped, showing that it had been made in 1942.

I took the re-barreled rifle to the gravel pit where I shot for the two years I lived at Beeville. It was in a poorly fitting stock. I started firing a load of 52 grains of IMR 4320 powder and 125-grain Sierra bullets. The rounds walked across the target from right to left as I shot. Then I noticed the fifth shot went where the fourth shot had gone and the next five after that went there, too. All seven were in a bumblebee, one-hole cluster.

I left there and went back to Bryan Dugat. For $10 I bought a used Model 70 stock he had on hand. I glassed the action and floated the barrel. After that I could not find a powder/bullet combination that would not shoot. Just so you understand, I mean that I have been able to get any commercial bullet and any commercial powder teamed together to shoot groups inside of an inch. Try that test with your pet rifle sometime.

Because of the success I had with cast bullets in pistols, I wanted to try cast bullets in my .30-06 rifle. I found at a store in Brownsville, Sturmers as I remember, a single cavity bullet mold #311299. I bought the mold, handles, 1,000 gas checks, and some bullet lubricant for $15. I had 200 pounds of salvaged pistol bullets picked up from the range at Amarillo. I took 100 pounds of salvaged material, added 3 percent tin, made a homogeneous mixture out of the whole 100 pounds, and started casting .30-caliber bullets.

I seated the gas checks with a hammer and finger lubricated the bullets. I started loading with Hodgdon 4227 powder behind the 205-grain cast bullet. Accuracy was excellent with loads up to 25 grains of powder. Then I tried Hodgdon 4895 and had equal success with loads up to 34 grains. Next I tried

4831 powder. Forty-six grains worked so well I never looked for another load. All of these loads were capable of staying inside of an inch at 100 yards.

A couple of years later Lyman came out with their 450 sizer lubricator. I got it with a .30 caliber die in .311 diameter. I had such success with the 311299 in an oversized condition I could not see squeezing it down much. The sized and lubricated bullets did not shoot any better, but they sure were easier to prepare and assemble and a lot less messy. In 1979 I had shot up the last of the 100-pound mix I had been using—some 3,000 rounds.

Just in case you wonder what purpose cast bullets in a rifle serve, let me state that I have successfully hunted at least the following varmints with cast bullets in that old Model 70: crows, armadillos, ground squirrels, rattlesnakes, nutria, coons, skunks, foxes, bobcats, coyotes, turtles, gars, and jack rabbits.

Also, let me state that cast bullets in that old .30-06 have also served me well in harvesting at least the following game animals: quail, turkey, cottontails, Barbados sheep, javelina, squirrels, spruce grouse, and deer. Let me also state that cast bullets allowed me to shoot more, which made me a better rifle shot than I would otherwise have been.

Rifle #565275 has been scoped with at least the following scopes over the years: a 3X Weaver, a 4X Weaver, a 6X Lyman, a 6X Leupold, and finally a 3X Lyman. Almost without exception the scopes have been in Weaver rings on Weaver bases. I also have hunted a great deal with this rifle using a Lyman 48 receiver sight. Until I was about fifty years old, I could shoot almost the same size groups with the receiver sight as with a scope at 100 yards. I owe G. R. Whittington and Tom Robinson a debt of gratitude for showing me the merits of a receiver sight.

At some point in time the aluminum trigger guard and floor plate of the featherweight were replaced with a steel set. I remember that happening about 1970. It is currently in its fifth stock. The present stock was taken off a .220 Swift that passed through my hands around 1978. It is pillar bedded, benchrest style, with the barrel floating.

If memory serves, a neighbor, Wayne Reinniger, became interested in the fairly new Hunter Class of the National Benchrest Rifle

Association in 1973 or 1974. He talked me into going to a shoot with him. After the shoot, I popped off and told Wayne that my Model 70 .30-06 would shoot with the best of the custom rifles represented there. Wayne snorted and told me I didn't know what I was talking about. I secured some Sierra and some Hornady 168-grain match bullets. I loaded them with 55 grains of H4831 powder. I chose that powder because of its cost to me (68¢ a pound). I chose 55 grains of it because it filled my LC63 match cases up to the base of the seated bullet.

I went to the rifle range out of San Marcos. I can remember Mr. French and Mr. Weide being there. I fired a 25-shot group with each bullet. Both 25-shot groups measured ¾ inch. At that time the rifle had a 4X Weaver Scope. Mr. French remarked that he thought they were most remarkable groups. I loaded 50 rounds with the Hornady bullets because they were cheaper.

I went to the next match at New Braunfels. As I remember, I fired a 50 the first relay, and they gave me $7.00 for winning it. The second relay I fired a 49. The third relay I fired a 50 but got out X-ed. The fourth I fired a 49. The fifth relay I fired a 50 and won it. They gave me $7.00 for winning the last relay, and more important they gave me twenty-five dollars for winning the match. By the way, that set a new range record for the 100-yard Hunter Class at New Braunfels. It was broken the next month, but it was the range record for a month. As a point of interest, three competitors at the match complained because partially burned granules of my 4831 powder were blowing back on them and disrupting their concentration. Kind of gives you the idea that 4831 is a little slow with a 168-grain bullet in a .30-06. Wonder what I could have done using 4350 powder?

The most memorable hunt I ever made was with 565275, a month backpack elk hunt in a wilderness area in Idaho in 1982. That hunt was the fulfillment of a thirty-year dream. A Speer 200-grain bullet pushed by 57 grains of Hodgdon 4831 enabled me to take a splendid mature bull elk. As I sit here at my desk in my private office and look up at his magnificent rack, I can get lost in a pleasant wave of memories. I finished up that hunt with my receiver sight on the rifle and cast bullets in the chamber for things like spruce grouse, marmot, snowshoe hair, and coyotes.

Since 1967 when I started shooting 565275, I have fired about 5,000 cast bullets and 5,000 jacket bullets through it. My groups have fallen off just a tad, but I really think it is me and old age and not the gun. It will still stay inside of an inch anytime I ask it to.

The most remarkable group I ever shot with the rifle was a 12-shot group. In 1974 I had just pillar bedded the rifle. I wanted to see how well it could shoot. On the first weekend of each month for a year, I would shoot one shot on a target from a cold, clean barrel. I kept that target. It measured just under an inch, center to center. Try that test on your pet rifle sometime!

In the years since I re-barreled 565275, it has furnished most of the meat that has been served at my table. It has done everything I have asked of it. Few who read this will ever experience the luxury of having a rifle that is so consistent that the shooter must accept responsibility every time a shot is missed. Since I re-barreled 565275 in 1967, no other person has ever fired a shot from it. I will probably maintain that practice until I have used up my allotted years to hunt.

Winchester called the Model 70 the rifleman's rifle. I am satisfied I own a 565275, the cream of the rifleman's rifles.

I now have a safe full of really fine center-fire rifles. They cover the full scope of rifle calibers from specialized varmint rifles to heavy big-game rifles. Each of these rifles is capable of firing groups under an inch, or I would not keep it. Funny thing though, because every time it really counts, ground squirrels to bear, I invariably reach for my faithful ol' .30-06.

When my time comes and someone scratches a hole in the ground for me, I may try to arrange to have 565275 thrown in with me. You know, just in case the American Indian was correct in his thoughts about hunting in an afterlife. Sure would not want to spend an eternity hunting with a sorry rifle, not when I could have taken 565275 with me!

Cold Trailing

Times change, people change, and conditions change. It is sad for me to look back at the changes I have hunted through. It is sad because not many of these changes have been to the benefit of the hunter or the animals he hunts.

In the past there have been years when I killed hundreds of quail in a year. I haven't killed a quail in eight years. In my part of the world the imported fire ant destroy most of the baby quail before they can leave the nest. Great stress is put on quail by the insecticides, herbicides, and fungicides used by the grain and cotton growers. They do not need the additional strain of my hunting them.

Turkey hunting has always been one of my favorite hunting activities. For years I would kill my limit, first in the winter season and later in the spring after Texas adopted a spring season. My home here used to have a healthy turkey population. The imported fire ant plus all their natural predators have all but eliminated my turkey flocks in the past eight years. I only see a couple of ancient turkeys now. I would as soon shoot an old human friend as shoot one of these old birds.

In the winter of 1942 Herbert Simons took me duck hunting on a lake in the forks of the Navidad and Lavaca Rivers. As I remember, that was about a ten-acre lake. By good sunrise I had crawled up in the brush at the edge of the lake. I potshot the sitting ducks in the closest bunch of mallards. As the thousands of ducks rose off the lake at my shot, they blotted out the light from the rising sun. With that one shot, I killed eight ducks. The ducks were that thick in the whole Texas Gulf Coast country. I continued to hunt ducks until about 1950. From then until 1980

I would only kill a few green wing and blue wing teal. Since 1980, I have not killed a duck. We have robbed her of her nesting grounds. We have weakened her with pesticides and toxic materials. The conditions under which a duck must survive are such that I cannot bring myself to kill one.

I ran foxes and coyotes with hounds in the early 1950s. Even then it was difficult to find a place to safely run ones hounds. Each year fewer ranchers would allow you to hunt on their places. I then changed to coonhounds because they could be hunted on smaller places. Each year saw the larger ranches broken up into smaller places. By 1970 it had become difficult to find enough land to run coons on. I then changed to beagles and ran cottontails and swamp rabbit. I own enough land to run my beagles on. Many of the fox and coyote hunters run foxes and coyotes in pens now. Many of the beagles in the eastern part of the United States run rabbits in pens. I will not run an animal in a pen.

Until eight years ago I shot rabbits over my pack of beagles regularly. Now I never kill a rabbit in front of my hounds. The imported fire ant destroys most of the baby rabbits while they are helpless in their nests. Then my fellow predators, the owls, hawks, coyotes, foxes, and bobcats must take their fair share of my rabbit crop. Consequently, there are only enough left for me to run with my hounds, certainly not enough for me to gun. I have hounds that are capable of running down a swamp rabbit and catching a good portion of the swamp rabbits they start. I try never to let that happen, and I am usually successful in catching the dogs off when I sense the rabbit is weakening.

In the years of 1965 and 1966 I completely shot out the barrels of two rifles, one a custom Mauser in what was then the wildcat cartridge .22-250, the other a Model 70 Winchester .270. Almost every shot fired from those rifles was fired at a prairie dog. I bought my powder for this shooting in fifty-pound kegs and my bullets and primers in lots of one thousand. I fired around ten thousand rounds from the .22-250 and seventy-five hundred rounds from the .270. Today, thanks to the "poison the prairie dog campaign" carried out by the federal government, farmers, and ranchers, I would be surprised to find a good healthy major prairie dog town in Texas.

I have not seriously fished since 1968. At that time my youngest son, Wade, asked me to take him float fishing on the San Marcos River. It had been four years since we had fished the San Marcos River, and he wanted to relive old memories. We floated in inner tubes with floating bait buckets and tackle boxes. We used ultralight spinning tackle. The last time we had fished that river was in the summer of 1964. At that time the San Marcos was pretty clear, pretty clean, and beautiful. On that fall day in 1968 I found the San Marcos River to be a cesspool, with more than a foot of sludge on the bottom. That filth came from the inadequate and faulty sewage system of the city of San Marcos, plus the runoff from a large cattle-feeding operation. I released the fish we caught and gave and traded my fishing tackle away. The salt waters along the Texas Gulf Coast are so fouled by the toxic material from the chemical plants along the coast, that I neither catch nor eat fish from those waters anymore. It would be unfair to give the chemical plants the whole blame for all the pollution there, but they more than contribute their share.

The last time I went elk hunting was in 1984 in a wilderness area in Idaho. I saw in easy rifle range the best bull elk I will probably ever see. He was a magnificent example of a mature bull elk. I lay and watched him for maybe five minutes before I lost sight of him in the brush. I even lined up the post cross hairs of the scope on my old .30-06 rifle on his heart/lung area. It would have been an easy shot from the solid rest on my backpack. I never touched the trigger. Expanding urban areas plus ever-increasing logging, ranching, and hunting pressure will in the future see the end of healthy elk herds. As I watched that splendid animal, I lost all desire to kill him.

Each year the urban areas infringe on the rural areas. The tendency is for ranches to get smaller. The smaller ranches place more and more stress on the deer population. I counted the hunters on the places that join my place. Each hunter can legally kill four deer per season. I counted eighteen hunters, who could kill seventy-two deer off of about five hundred acres. That would amount to a deer for each seven acres. We do not have a deer population that would sustain taking a deer to each seven acres. I now only kill one deer each year. I usually choose a doe who has developed a taste for the beans on my garden fence or one who hankers for my peaches, plums, pears, or melons. That one doe amounts to almost all the meat Billye and I eat.

It might appear to you that I am in the process of joining the ANTI-HUNTING group. Let me set you straight on that. I killed a possum year before last because he was eating my cantaloupes. I have killed five coons in the past five years, three because they were eating my cow feed, one because he was eating my watermelons, and one because Ol' Scruffy, my main lady beagle, treed him. That coon, by the way, cost me $485.00 because after Scruffy and I killed him, I let a "dead" coon bite me—which meant that I had to take rabies shots. I also killed four or five armadillos, all with a Ruger .32 Magnum pistol because they were damaging drought-stressed oak trees around my house. Finally, one day last spring while Billye was in town for the day, I shot two young fox squirrels between my house and the dog pens, strictly on impulse. I head shot them with a fine little Winchester .22 rimfire rifle. I dressed them, rolled them in flour, fried them, made cream gravy from the dregs, and set back and gorged myself. Hot damn! They were good.

For the most part I now satisfy my need to hunt by running my beagles on swamp rabbits. I maintain two packs, a fast pack and a slow pack. My fast pack is made up of dogs from a family that I have bred for generations. They are a fine pack of hounds. My slow pack are all directly from old friend, Don Garrett of Bryan. His idea not mine. They, too, are in their own way a fine pack of rabbit hounds. I run at least one of my packs of beagles almost every day. In order for me to enjoy running my beagles, I must be in good enough condition to stay with them throughout the race.

For this reason I condition myself by running six or seven miles every other day about daylight. I have been running to condition myself for hunting since I was forty-six years old. I have been able to ask my body to respond to some rigorous conditions in the past ten years. It pleases me that because of my conditioning, my old body keeps coming through for me when I ask it to, flat low-lands or mountains, hot or cold, wet or dry.

The things that bother me most as an aging hunter, are loss of hearing, loss of sight, and loss of eye-hand coordination. These losses rob me of my hunting abilities. There is no way for me to compensate for these losses, nor am I able to maintain them at their present levels. It is a slow, gradual, never-ending process. I abhor it, but like a cold, wet camp hunt, there is nothing I can do about it but just hunker up and take it.

I have been blessed for a lifetime with wonderful country to hunt. I have paid to hunt only once in my life. That was a two-year lease for deer hunting. I paid for that strictly so my oldest son, Tom, would have a place to deer hunt. All the rest of my hunting, be it hounds or guns, varmints or game, fowl or fish, has been as free as a gentle breeze or a sunset. In my heart I recognize a huge debt of gratitude to all those who allowed me free access to their land. These people stretch from Texas to New Mexico, from New Mexico to Colorado, from Colorado to Idaho, from Idaho to Oregon, from Oregon to Wyoming and from Wyoming to Oklahoma. The full list of people would fill a filing cabinet.

I also, compliments of the U.S. government, had the opportunity of deepwater fishing in the Gulf of Mexico. The government was considerate enough to even issue me a captain for my ship who before the war had been a commercial fisherman. Before that the government was even considerate enough to send me to an island in the Pacific so that I could fish there. That island was two hundred yards wide and three hundred yards long. They let me stay there thirteen months, with no chance to leave. That island was twenty-six miles from Kwajalein in the Marshall Islands. Then the government was thoughtful enough to send me to a tiny island thirty miles from Makin in the Gilbert Islands; they let me stay there nine months. They even furnished Gilbertese natives who gave me my graduate work in South Pacific fishing. So you can see I have even had the U.S. government looking out for all the right places for me to fish.

As I look to the future, I can see nothing but a bleak horizon for the hunter of the future. The outlook for fishing is bleak indeed. In time our fishing waters will become so contaminated with industrial waste, human waste, and agricultural waste that they will not support gamefish life. The fisherman will have to go to a fish farm and fish out of a fish pen. The outlook for the bird hunter is just as dreary as for fishermen. Because of the toll taken by pollution, loss of cover, and fire ants, he will be forced to shoot released, pen-raised birds whether they be quail, pheasants, turkeys, or ducks. The deer hunter will shoot a penned-up animal. He will be taken out and an animal will be chosen for him to shoot depending upon his ability to pay. This already is the way business is done on some places now; not only deer but some transplanted African and Asian animals as well. Elk hunting will follow the same path.

I go to a livestock auction barn every once in a while to sell or buy a calf, cow or bull. I see tame ram Barbados sheep sell for ten times their value so that they can be placed out for some "hunter" to shoot and have the head mounted for display as a hunting trophy. I see domestic horned billy goats sell for fifteen times their value so they can be placed out to be shot and the head mounted.

I see deer, elk, sheep, antelope, and javelina heads mounted and displayed to show what a mighty hunter the person displaying the head is. The contest between the game animal and the hunter is to me a personal, private thing. To me it is degrading to the animal and to the hunter to hang the head out for public display. It makes me a little sick to my stomach. Be that as it may, I think I will puke the first time I see a damn domestic goat or sheep head mounted for display. They are there. I just hope I never see one.

If you have stayed with me this far, you probably realize it is time to put out the fire, catch up the dogs and go to the house. Before I do, let me make one comment. In this year of 1995, I have been blessed for forty-five years with a wife who my youngest son, Wade, said was the only human on this earth who could have tolerated me. I have taken this beautiful, generous, loving lady, and abused her in every way a hunter could. In times when money was a problem I have taken dollars that should have gone for shoes for the children, food for the table, or payment for the doctor and spent it on "just one more hound." In times of her need for support, comfort, and solace, I have loaded up and left for a little bird hunt or deer hunt. For fun and games I have given her the opportunity to go and camp in the open in the rough with me where it is always too hot or too cold, too wet or too dry, too windy or too still, with always too many mosquitoes, chiggers, ticks, snakes, and always away from the crowd. I am almost never lonesome or feel a need for social contact, and it is most difficult for me to try to adjust to her social needs. I have a tendency not to talk much and by nature could go for days without much if any conversation. Silence too is an abuse.

If marriage could be equated to a heavy load carried by two people, I have to say Billye has always picked up the heavy end. I hope she knows I love her, and I think she does. This person who I married as a child in 1950, who has developed into a little, independent, gray-haired grandmother in 1995, is the person I most respect and admire in this world. I hope she knows that, but I doubt she does. I wish I could make up to her in some way for all of my failings, but I am neither perceptive enough nor disciplined enough to be able to do that. I can only hope I'm lucky enough to be able to stumble through the rest of my life with her.

Billye knows what a hunter is now. I'll bet on that fall day in 1949 when we first met, had she known what a hunter was and that I was a hunter, she would have turned her back and walked away. I sure could not have faulted her if she had.

Well, enough of my drivel. Shoot man, I have a litter of pups that need starting!